PACTS:

The Coalition for Change

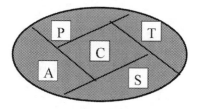

HOW ONE DISTRICT'S EFFORT TO CHANGE
COULD HELP YOU BUILD A BETTER SCHOOL

by

Bill Collins

THE SISYPHUS FOUNDATION, INC.

iUniverse books may be ordered through booksellers or by contacting:

iUniverse
1663 Liberty Drive
Bloomington, IN 47403
www.iuniverse.com
844-349-9409

Because of the dynamic nature of the Internet, any web addresses or links contained in
this book may have changed since publication and may no longer be valid. The views
expressed in this work are solely those of the author and do not necessarily reflect the
views of the publisher, and the publisher hereby disclaims any responsibility for them.

Any people depicted in stock imagery provided by Getty Images are
models, and such images are being used for illustrative purposes only.
Certain stock imagery © Getty Images.

ISBN: 978-1-4502-6883-7 (sc)
ISBN: 978-1-4502-6885-1 (hc)
ISBN: 978-1-4502-6884-4 (e)

Print information available on the last page.

iUniverse rev. date: 09/07/2023

Abstract

This case study chronicles the efforts of one urban high school district in Northern California to implement the guidelines of the *Mathematics Framework for California Public Schools*. It quantifies surveyed responses solicited from parents, administrators, curriculum leaders, teachers, and students in the district. The case study also assesses their level of agreement on issues relating to mathematics reform. These agents of change constitute the PACTS Coalition. As such, they generally agree that mathematics is a tough subject and that it should be fun; however, their level of agreement vacillates when the investigation turns to issues such as ability level grouping, the incorporation of diversity, and the question of "inclusion." In general, members of the alliance believe that the effect of reform efforts has been deleterious to the overall quality of mathematics education at their school site, and in the district. Many respondents cite poor communication, ineffectual leadership, and a lack of direction as chief deterrents to effective mathematics reform; most agree that cohesion, unity, and morale among the mathematics staff in the district have suffered as a result. Now, like "the blind men and the elephant," we show that the varying perspectives of the PACTS Coalition is key to recognizing the complexity of educational issues while revealing, with simplicity, the beauty and the vision needed for lasting education reform.

About the Author

...Why Me?

Over the course of my career in education, I took on many roles: teacher, mathematics department chair, curriculum leader, project director, program administrator, master's student, master teacher, author, and most important of all, parent. And though I embraced each new responsibility as it came, I was never quite able to forget or to let go of the old. At times, I struggled to reconcile why one role seemed to be at odds, or in conflict, with another. For me, the levels of interaction, interplay, and synergistic relationships among the various roles and duties were palpable; measurable and real. My ongoing struggle led me to the conclusion that before real reform in education could take place, these conflicts must be reconciled: in me, within each of us, among all of us. Ultimately, that led me to this study: *PACTS: The Coalition for Change.* It is my hope that my journey and reflections may be of assistance to you as you advance through your career, pursue meaningful education reform, or seek to build a better school!

Acknowledgments

This work is dedicated to my mother, Mrs. Elizabeth H. Collins—my first and lifelong teacher. May my work speak for me as yours did for you.

I also wish to thank Dr. John Hathaway and Dr. Barbara Z. Dawson for your help and assistance (Special thanks, Z, for keeping my feet firmly on the ground.).

I wish to thank my wife, Lorena, and children Raylene, Preston and Justin for completing my "circle of life"; and, for providing me the encouragement, peace, and sustenance needed to see this project through to the end.

I wish to acknowledge the dedicated staff and faculty of the Elizabeth Union High School District for their trust and participation. I trust you find this work worthy of your input and helpful in your continuing pursuit of excellence. Also, I wish to thank the Superintendent of the Elizabeth Union High School District for your support and encouragement; without which, this study could not have been done.

Table of Contents

List of Figures

Introduction

A Statement of the Problem

In 1985, the California Department of Education drafted the *Mathematics Framework for California Public Schools* in response to national criticism regarding the plight of the American public education system. The *Framework* was to provide direction, guidelines, and leadership to local school districts in their attempts to improve schools. Like many other districts in the state, the Elizabeth Union High School District[1] made major changes to its mathematics curriculum and methods of instruction in response to the *Framework*. The purpose of this study is to assess the changes made to the mathematics curriculum in the Elizabeth Union High School District in light of the *California State Mathematics Framework*. The study intends to determine whether the district's efforts to implement state's guidelines worked to meet the needs of its students.

Overview

In 1983, the national report, *A Nation at Risk*, sounded an alarm on the state of the American public schools. It blamed schools for failing to prepare American youth to compete in an ever increasing global marketplace. After its publication, many other reports joined

---

1 pseudonym

the call for dramatic change in the American educational system and the 1980s became a decade of reform. Many states joined the call for change by passing education-reform acts. Their aim was to leverage control and to force improvements of schools at the district level. Because mathematics was viewed as key to opportunity in this global marketplace, criticism of mathematics education in America was particularly harsh.

In 1985, the California Department of Education drafted and adopted the *Mathematics Framework for California Public Schools.* The *Framework* set guidelines that districts were to follow to improve mathematics instruction and to provide an equal opportunity for success for all of California's diverse student population. The Elizabeth Union High School District in Northern California was one of those districts.

Along with the national call for change came many tangential concerns regarding the nation's goals and standards. In 1990, the President and state governors proclaimed six national education goals to improve schools and student achievement by the year 2000. The National Council of Teachers of Mathematics issued the *Curriculum and Evaluation Standards* (1989). The *Standards* asked mathematics teachers to go beyond "basic skills" to emphasize problem solving, understanding, and meaningful communication about mathematics. In California, schools were required to align their mathematics curriculum to the *Model Curriculum* standards every three years.

Because of the magnitude and systemic nature of the change prescribed by the national reports, many agencies were involved; consequently, there were many "agents of change." On the national level, the President provided leadership and direction. In 1993, the president signed the first bill setting national goals for American schools. The National Science Foundation and the Carnegie Commission were among the agencies that led the way on issues of school reform. At the state level, legislatures, colleges, and universities assumed leadership roles in teacher education, training, and licensing. Locally, grass root committees took active roles in the improvement of schools in their community. Parents, administrators, curriculum leaders, teachers, and students formed *ad hoc* committees to forge curriculum reform. The question aroused: Could this interplay of centralized and grass roots reform yield excellence and improve the American education system?

To explore this question, this study assessed the efforts of one school district in Northern California to meet the guidelines set forth by the state's *Mathematics Framework*. The purpose of this study was to determine whether the district's efforts and the state's guidelines worked in concert or in conflict to meet the needs of its students.

The Clarion Call

The "Nature of Reform"

The Call for Change The student population in America is changing. Surely, you have heard this refrain before. By the year 2000, one in every three American students was of minority descent. By 2020, America as a whole will face the oxymoronic minority-majority student population that some of its states and many of its local communities have come to know so well. Minorities will become the majority of students in the United States. (*Everybody Counts*, 1989).

It is this changing population that America will have to feed, clothe, employ, but first and foremost, educate if it is to maintain its position of leadership into the twenty-first century. It is this changing population that will bring to the classrooms of tomorrow educational skills and abilities as wide and as diverse as their backgrounds. And, it is this changing population, for many of whom English will be a second language, that will place even greater demands on an already burdened public education system.

The report, *A Nation at Risk*, blamed schools for failing to develop the human resources needed by American industry to compete successfully in the international marketplace. Beginning with its publication in 1983, the 1980s became the decade of school reform (Pajek, 1993). The call for reform of the public education system in America was echoed on national, state, and local levels.

Many reports criticized schools for not keeping pace with changes in society and technology (Pajek, 1993). The National Assessment of Educational Progress (NAEP) issued several reports revealing that the majority of students are not developing intellectual capacities necessary to democratic citizenship, lifelong learning, and productive employment in the economic system (Melissa, Owens, and Phillips, 1990). Because mathematics was viewed as a key to opportunity and careers, criticism of mathematics education in America was particularly severe (*Everybody Counts*, 1989).

Many states responded to the criticism by passing education-reform acts that included heavy doses of top-down management and tighter regulation [Berry and Ginsburg cited in Pajek (1993)]. In California, where over one-half of the state's public school students are non-white, the State Department of Education adopted the *Mathematics Framework for California Public Schools* (1985). The *Framework*, extended in 1992, sought to address the needs of California's changing student population. It called for changes in the mathematics curriculum and the delivery of mathematics instruction to meet the needs, and different learning styles, of students from diverse backgrounds. It recommended the formation of Math A, Math B, and Math C courses: A sequence of integrated mathematics courses which placed greater emphasis on "hands-on" manipulatives and "cooperative learning groups." In 1988, the California Department of Education initiated the development of the Math A course to replace ninth-grade general mathematics (1992). This new experimental curricula was founded on the notion that teachers and learners, together, would build projects to understand more deeply the problems that grow from their lived experience (Schubert, 1993).

To create the first of these courses, Math A, the California State Department of Education sent out guidelines throughout the state seeking those interested in designing and submitting units to create the new curriculum. In designing Math A units, the guidelines suggested that each unit start from an overriding real-life situation, have compelling and difficult problems, and contain key mathematical ideas which emanate from basic themes. Would-be course developers were encouraged to not feel restricted to the topics listed—but feel free to explore and share ideas. Units accepted by the California Department of Education were "gathered together and edited by the state committees to produce a well-balanced course" (Lester, 1989). State policymakers hoped that the developmental units would also be used in Math B and Math C in the transitional years of defining those courses.

Local school districts throughout the state responded to the call for change. The Elizabeth Union High School District, one of the largest secondary high school districts in the state, was among them. This district, which is comprised of ten comprehensive schools and one continuation school, is located in a large urban community in Northern California. It was a district undergoing rapid change in its student population, high failure rates in its remedial level mathematics classes, and low minority enrollment in its upper level mathematics classes. Driven by a sincere desire to do a better job, district policymakers embraced the call for change [Subject Area Coordinator (SAC) Interview, 1994]. So, under the direction of the Math Subject Area Coordinator, and guided by the principles outlined in the *Framework*, grass root committees of teachers developed Elizabeth District Math A materials.

Over the course of the decade, Remedial Math and Introduction to Algebra courses in the district were phased out, eliminated, or dropped to be replaced with Math A. When state materials were not ready, or in some cases deemed not at an appropriate level for Elizabeth Union High School District students, district Math A materials were used (SAC Interview, 1994). When the transition to the new curriculum in the Elizabeth Union High School District was complete, of the 164 sections of non-college preparatory mathematics offered in the district during the 1993-1994 school year, only 13 (8%) were text-based Introduction to Algebra.

However, all educators in the district did not heed the call for change. Traditional mathematics teachers in the district were not enthusiastic about placing great emphasis on curriculum development. They claimed that the mathematics curriculum was already developed; it was merely a matter of providing students with what was known. They pointed to many factors other than the curriculum which contributed to students' poor performance in mathematics: poor attendance, lack of motivation, unpreparedness, and weak basic skills. They questioned the central assumption that curriculum reform was somehow enhanced by grass roots participation. Many traditional teachers did not see the need for using state or district produced units, over which they felt no "ownership" and little control, in place of material they could develop themselves based on their individual need. They wondered, like others before them, could this interplay of centralized and grass roots reform yield excellence, equity, and genuine human growth (Klein 1991; Beyer and Apple 1988). Many units were not used; boxes piled up in mathematics storage centers only to become scratch paper. Morale and unity of mathematics departments throughout the district were strained by this issue.

Like many critics of the experimentalist position, which is quite dominant among curriculum theorist today, the traditionalists of the district thought it impossible, impractical, and too costly to think about building a curriculum for each learner (Schubert, 1993). Perhaps their voices were heard: During the 1994-95 school year, the Elizabeth Union High School District abandoned its efforts to implement the Math A and Math B curricula proposed by the *California State Mathematics Framework* and mandated algebra for all of its incoming freshmen.

The Goals of Change There has been general agreement among educators, legislators, business leaders, and the general public that the time has come to improve our schools and to support calls for sweeping reforms in the American educational system. Although most involved agree that there is the need for change, there has been less agreement as to the goals of change. Even where goals have been stated, objectives written, and plans developed for fundamental change on national, state, and local levels, many legitimate questions have been raised concerning the purpose and attainment of these goals.

The student population in America is indeed changing. Present and future trends in higher education reveal that people of color in the United States are a dramatically increasing but seriously undereducated segment in society ("Pursuing Diversity," 1991). As predicted, by 2000 minorities accounted for roughly thirty percent of the population. Government and industry alike have noted the potential economic effect of these alarming trends in education. With continued projected increases in minority population, the situation threatens to affect the national economy: Given the present level of minority education, the potential shortage of qualified workers equipped to meet the needs of the market is a serious concern (Economist 1990b; Hodgkinson, 1983).

During the 1980s, National Assessment of Education Progress (NAEP) issued several reports on student achievement that showed most 17-year-olds have serious gaps in their knowledge of core academic subject. Of greater significance in today's global market, NAEP's reports revealed that students in the United States ranked near the bottom among economically developed countries on international assessments of their knowledge of mathematics and science (NAEP, 1990).

In February 1990, the President and state governors proclaimed a set of six national education goals to prompt profound improvements in schools and student achievement by the year 2000. Briefly stated, the six national goals for education are as follows: (1) by the year 2000, all children will start school ready to learn; (2) 90% of high school students will graduate; (3) students will be competent in basic subjects and exhibit responsible citizenship; (4) U.S. students will lead the world in mathematics and science; (5) every American adult will be literate; and (6) schools will be drug-free and safe ("National goal," 1990). In March, 1994, the Goals 2000 bill was signed ("Clinton signs," 1994).

The National Council of Teachers of Mathematics (NCTM) joined the call to set national goals and standards to improve mathematics education in America. The NCTM's *Curriculum and Evaluation Standards* (NCTM, 1989) asked teachers to go beyond an emphasis on "basic skills" of computation to emphasize problem solving, understanding, and meaningful communication about mathematics (Putnam & Geist, 1994). Because of the noted changes in the minority makeup of the American school population, a wide range of national educational and child advocacy organizations recommended the abolition of tracking. They reasoned that too often tracking creates class and race-linked differences in access to learning. They claimed that because of the inequities in opportunity it creates, tracking is a major contributor to the continuing gaps in achievement between disadvantaged and affluent students and between minorities and whites (Oakes, 1985, 1992).

In California, where the rate of growth in the minority student population was as great as, or greater than, anywhere else in the nation, the 1983 California Legislature enacted Senate Bill 813 (a far-reaching reform measure designed to improve financing, curriculum, textbooks, testing, and teacher and administrator training in the state's elementary and secondary schools). As a result of this Bill, the Department of Education drafted the *Model Curriculum Standards* (1985). Inspired by the position advanced by the Carnegie Foundation for the Advancement of Teaching that "the curriculum has a core," the Standards were intended to "underscore the fact that a partnership between the state and local school district is crucial to making [the state's] schools the best in the nation" (p 3).

In 1985, the Department of Education also adopted the *California State Framework in Mathematics* (1985). This visionary framework called for changes in the delivery of mathematics instruction to multicultural students based on the "discovery" of mathematical concepts and principles. Along with the new *Framework* and *Model Standards* came the need for new tests and assessments. In this climate of change the California Assessment Test, which had relied on multiple choice responses, was now questioned by many policymakers. New "authentic" tests that allowed for open-ended responses and evaluation were developed and put in place. In 1987-88, the state experimented with giving open-ended mathematics items in the 12th grade level. In 1993-94 school year, the new CAP test (later known as the California Learning Assessment Test or CLAS test) was given statewide (Grant, Peterson, & Shojgreen-

Downer, 1994). Local school districts were required to align their curriculum to the new framework and encouraged to compare their curriculum to the model standards at least once every three years.

The Elizabeth Union High School District, like other districts in the state, was faced with increased societal demands and limited resources. It took immediate steps to rethink and to redesign many of its instructional approaches in light of the *State Framework* and *Model Curriculum Standards.* Exceedingly familiar with the needs of a diverse student population, the district set out to align its curriculum along the guidelines put forth by the state. In its mission statement, the district echoed the view of national and state policymakers that the diversity of the student population required changes in the curriculum. Its goal was to make the curriculum more inclusive of cultures and to train its staff to provide them a better understanding of diversity. The district sought to prepare students for a more competitive job market, and to encourage and prepare more students so that they could pursue post-secondary education. The district recognized that it had to provide a safe, secure learning environment and assistance to students and their families with social and personal problems ("Academic, personal," 1993). Many of its ten high schools took steps toward restructuring their curriculum, eliminating tracking, expanding magnet and academy programs, and integrating technology in portions of their curriculum.

But with the advent of each national, state, or local goal and standard came questions and concerns. While a recent Gallup Poll of 1,594 adults showed widespread support for national goals, citizens questioned the role of parents, state, and local communities in the attainment of those goals (Elam, 1990). Concerns were also raised concerning funding and national tests. And what about teachers? Will a national certification system be necessary to assure that quality teachers are prepared and skilled? Many states, already concerned about increased demand and limited funds, looked to "parental choice initiatives" and "voucher systems" as ways to spur competition and improve the quality of their schools. State colleges and universities were also involved. Many, through national and private funding, began designing new curricula, teacher pre-service, and assessment tools for high school mathematics. Local communities, recognizing that constant community involvement is critical to meeting the goals of safe, drug-free, learning environments set out to develop their own plans for improvement of their school. Each community examined the national goals in light of the needs of its children and families; consequently, many communities across the nation resisted risking their children's future on untested ideas. In California, the CLAS test came under attack for being psychologically invasive, too subjective, and too difficult to score (Guido, 1994). In September 1994, the governor of California vetoed the bill which would have extended funding for the controversial testing program (Aratani, 1994). With this, the question remained: Could national standards, formulated necessarily by authorities who live outside of a specific context for which they are making curricular policy, fit the needs and interest of people who live in those contexts? (Schubert, 1993).

A related concern was the misrepresentation of course content. The fall newsletter of the Mathematics Diagnostic Testing Project (1994) cited a "case where a university student who could not graph a line admitted to her pre-calculus instructor that although she had received a 'B' grade in AP Calculus, the course had been calculus 'in name only'" (p. 1). The newsletter goes on to state that "by so doing, [the school] violated the trust of the students consigned to its care, as well as the entire academic community." To this day, one of the major constraints to real school reform is the lack of consensus about why reform is badly needed and what changes are most central (Cawelti, 1993).

The Agents of Change The national call for change in the American educational system, trumpeted by the national report, *A Nation at Risk*, had many voices; thus, many "agents of change." It was societal and political reform at its roots. Business and political leaders wanted the United States to be competitive with the Japanese in today's global marketplace. Agencies, both public and private, issued reports critical of schools for not preparing our students for a global information economy they will inherit. State officials expanded monitoring of local schools, and state agencies designed new programs to toughen processes of teacher certification and evaluation (Berry, Ginsburg, 1990). Colleges and universities, trainers of tomorrow's teachers and today's youths, were actively involved. Business leaders' involvement in school reform at the state and local levels began to shape the agenda of schooling and educational leadership during the 1980s. By the late 1980s, an image of the successful educational leaders as "corporate visionary" was prominent (Pajek, 1993). Many public officials had come to believe that what's good for business is good for schools (Cuban, 1993).

In California, assessment, curriculum and instruction, staff development, diversity, and state/district/school action were systematically linked. Over the past decade, the California State Legislature took steps to improve its educational system with passage of Senate Bill 813, the adoption of the *California Model and Standard*, and the *California State Mathematics Framework*. The state superintendent of schools leveraged system-wide support for change through state department control of testing, textbooks, and teacher education. State policymakers believed that they could steer school practice and change school outcomes (Ball, Cohen, 1990). To assure continued funding, school districts across the state worked to implement the changes and to meet new guidelines and mandates.

In the Elizabeth Union High School District, a concerted effort was made to align the mathematics curriculum to the guidelines set forth by the *California State Mathematics Framework*. Throughout the district, to varying degrees, district and school site committees of parents, administrators, curriculum leaders (scholars, developers, researchers), teachers, and students worked to revise curricula. Attempts were made to integrate computers across the curriculum, to develop problem solving skills in all students, and to develop citizenship and teamwork with the infusion of cooperative learning. Concurrent with these attempts, an effort was made in the district to address multiculturalism and diversity through the curriculum by responding to *all* students in the classroom while monitoring performance of said students ("Academic, personal," 1993). These complex changes required great commitment, motivation and belief by those being asked to carry them out and relied upon the efforts of many people working insightfully on the solution and committing themselves to concentrated action together (Fullan, 1993).

The Coalition for Change According to Schlechty in *Schools for the 21st Century*, for effective change to occur, five functions must be fulfilled. First, the nature of change must be conceptualized. Second, people must be made aware of the change. Third, those not involved must be called on for support, and where possible incorporated in the change process. Fourth, people must be motivated to act in the direction indicated by the change. And finally, a system of ongoing support and training must be provided for those who are being asked to support the change (Schlechty, 1990).

In the Elizabeth Union High School District, various groups of parents, administrators, curriculum leaders (in this study: the mathematics department chairs and the Subject Area Coordinator), teachers, and students worked to implement the changes outlined by the state *Framework*. Their goal was to bring about effective change in the educational system as they operated as agents of change within the context of the following broadly defined roles:

> PARENT: The child's first and lifelong teacher; provider of a safe home and learning environment.

> ADMINISTRATOR: Policymaker who sets the curriculum in the school and provides teacher-support services.

> CURRICULUM LEADER: Advocate for the curriculum. Department policymaker who acts as the liaison between the administrator and teacher.

> TEACHER: Instructor who sets the curriculum and the policy in the classroom.

> STUDENT: Learner who must depend on others to provide the support, environment, and tools necessary for success.

In any district, it is the strength of the alliance between and among parents, administrators, curriculum leaders, teachers, and students (PACTS) which determines the success or failure of its reform efforts. By PACTS, the researcher refers to the deep-structure "fabric of relations" interwoven between and among parents, administrators, curriculum leaders, teachers, and students on a campus. This coalition, with the curriculum at its core, is key to effective and sustainable school reform (see Figure 1).

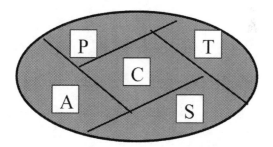

Figure 1 The PACTS Coalition.

To build strong coalitions for change all agents of change must work together to raise their levels of awareness, agreement, and commitment on the issues of change. Fullan (1993) suggests that "synergy of curriculum, technology, teacher development, assessment, structure and governance, and school-external agencies" is a "winning design" and a way to direct future reform efforts. The intent of this research is to examine the synergistic relations between and among the agents of change in the Elizabeth Union High School District, and to measure their levels of awareness, agreement, and commitment to issues of systemic mathematics reform.

Methods

Introduction

In March 1992, the researcher received permission from the Elizabeth District superintendent to conduct a study of the district's efforts to implement the guidelines of the *California State Mathematics Framework*. The research was conducted during the following 1993-94 school year. In November 1993, the researcher attended a district Mathematics Coordinators' Committee meeting to inform the mathematics curriculum leaders (department chairs) and the mathematics Subject Area Coordinator of the purpose of the study and solicited their support. In December 1993, the researcher attended a Principals' Meeting to inform this group of the study, the Superintendent's endorsement, and to request their cooperation and support. In January 1994, letters were sent to all district mathematics personnel to formally introduce the researcher, to inform them of the study, and to present each mathematics department member with an opportunity to influence the direction of the study through suggestions and/or questions. Some responses to the introductory letter were incorporated in the survey statements.

Subjects

Within one school district, five groups participated in the study: administrators, teachers, curriculum leaders, students, and parents.

All five groups of participants completed questionnaires. In addition, the group of mathematics curriculum leaders and the mathematics Subject Area Coordinator were interviewed. The administrators in the study consisted of ten principals and twenty-five associate principals. All of the district's 132 mathematics teachers were asked to participate in the study. The curriculum leaders consisted of the thirteen mathematics department chairs and the one subject area coordinator. The student sample was selected from existing mathematics classes. Ten mathematics classes from each of ten high schools, for a total of 100 mathematics classes, were included. Teachers gave their consent to the researcher to survey their class. Of the ten classes surveyed at each site, five were college preparatory classes and five were non-college preparatory classes. Whenever possible, classes were screened based on being "pre-*Framework*" or "post-*Framework*." The "pre-*Framework*" classes were those classes taught in the district before publication of the *California State Mathematics Framework* (1985), and post-*Framework* classes were those created and introduced to the district in response to *Framework*. Parents of only those students selected to participate in the study made up the parent sample space. A random sampling of fifty parents from each of ten schools (total of 500 parents) was surveyed. Because the parents were identified and linked to the students by class, the parent surveys necessarily span the same types and levels of mathematics classes as the student surveys.

Materials

Three questionnaires, each consisting of twenty-five statements gleaned from the *California State Mathematics Framework* (1985, 1992), related articles, teacher suggestions, and other sources were constructed. One of the three questionnaires was administered to each of the five groups of participants. Educators (administrators, curriculum leaders, and teachers) were given the same questionnaire. Parents and students were given different questionnaires; each with statements tailored to fit their respective points of view. Statements on the surveys were cross-referenced by number and each statement related to a topic, issue, or theme of the mathematics curriculum reform movement. Educator, parent, and student surveys had at most fifteen questions in common. Survey statements were sometimes referred to as questions because the researcher believed that participants were more likely to answer "questions" than to respond to "statements." Respondents were able to add comments, questions, or suggestions about the survey at the end of the survey.

Procedure

Surveys were pretested for design flaws and errors. Then, ten classes from each of ten high schools in the district were surveyed. Classes were selected based on their level of mathematics, whether they were college preparatory or not, and whether they were offered in the district before the publication of the 1985 *Mathematics Framework* or not. The same researcher administered the survey to all classes. The researcher was consistent in the instructions and directions given to each class. Questionnaires took approximately twenty minutes to complete. Principals received the administrators' survey by hand and were asked to pass them on to their on-site associates; curriculum leaders (thirteen department chairs and one subject area coordinator) received their survey at one of their monthly coordinators' meetings; teachers received their survey through the district mail. All educators were asked to return their survey through the district's mail system in an envelope that was provided. Finally, 500 parents were surveyed. Parents received the survey by mail and were provided a stamped, self-addressed envelope for the return of the survey. On the surveys, all participants were asked to indicate the extent to which they agreed or disagreed with various statements regarding issues of mathematics reform. Participants were informed by a cover letter that the survey was anonymous and that "no one will ever know what their individual responses are." During the course of the research, all curriculum leaders were interviewed. They were asked to respond to a list of questions designed to garner information regarding the mathematics program at their site. The information they provided was used to tabulate the course offerings, types, textbooks, and materials used at each school site during the 1993-94 school year.

Delimitations

This study was conducted in a large, urban school district. It chronicles the "Nature of Reform" as perceived by this district's parents, administrators, curriculum leaders, teachers, and students; its various "agents of change." The study consisted of the surveyed responses from one school district: ten comprehensive high schools, 132 mathematics teachers, thirty-five site administrators, thirteen mathematics department chairs, and one Subject Area Coordinator. Also, it consisted of student survey responses taken by random from a representative sample of 100 mathematics classes (approximately 2200 students), and respondents to parent surveys solicited from 500 parents.

Results

Purpose

The purpose of this report was to assess the changes made to the mathematics curriculum in the Elizabeth Union High School District and to examine whether the district's efforts to meet state's guidelines worked to the betterment or to the detriment of its students.

Background

The Elizabeth Union High School District is a large urban school district in Northern California. It is comprised of ten comprehensive high schools and one continuation high school. Its 22,000 student population is representative of the multicultural diversity that exists in California. It is one of the largest high school districts in the state. The Elizabeth Union High School District has long faced the issues of change and diversity that were the focus of the nation during 1980s. Over the past decade, the district had taken many steps to confront the issue of change and prepare its students for the twenty-first century. In addition, there were a number of special projects and programs that were prominent in the district which addressed the need for improvement in students' success in mathematics. The researcher feels compelled to comment on two of them at this time.

Equity 2000 Project When this research was being conducted, the Elizabeth Union High School District had entered an agreement with the College Board to participate in the Equity 2000 Project: a coalition of schools, postsecondary institutions, state agencies, foundations, and other associations whose stated goal is "to increase dramatically the number of poor and minority students who attend and succeed in college." The Equity 2000 Project, based on research commissioned and published by the College Board, found that all students who plan to attend college and take geometry in high school go to college regardless of race or ethnicity. As a result, the Project designated Algebra I and geometry as "gateway" courses to college success. Due, in part, to its alliance with the Equity 2000 Project, policymakers in the Elizabeth Union High School District mandated "algebra for all" incoming freshmen during the 1994-95 school year. This alarmed many of the mathematics teachers in the district. They were quite aware that a statement and its converse are not necessarily true. Teachers were concerned that by "forcing" students to take algebra and geometry who may not want to, or worse, who may not be prepared, the results portend disaster and will certainly not lead to students choosing to go to college.

The researcher wishes to reemphasize that the focus of this study was the impact the *California State Mathematics Framework* on the Elizabeth Union High School District. It was specifically designed to that end. That notwithstanding, the researcher recognizes that the atmosphere in the Elizabeth Union High School District was charged with the talk of change, and that many participants spoke specifically to the implementation of the special program: Equity 2000. In fact, this lead one student to comment on his/her survey:

> What, no mention of the dreaded Equity 2000? Is this what your [*sic*] trying to get us to say yes to reform? Do you believe Equity 2000 is true reform? Is this a way for you to have us say yes we want reform so you can implement Equity 2000?

It was not.

In fact, the concept of Equity 2000 prevailed, and is still at work in the district today. All incoming freshmen in the Elizabeth School District are placed in Algebra; the questions and concerns regarding the wisdom of that policy also persist to this day.

The Jose Valdes Institute The Jose Valdes Institute is the vision of one of the most celebrated teachers in the Elizabeth Union High School District and is named in his honor. Founded in 1989, it is funded in part by the Packard Foundation and the Elizabeth Union High School District. It is a program dedicated to increasing the enrollment and success of minority students, particularly Hispanics and African-Americans, in mathematics. It, too, is predicated on the belief that all students can do mathematics. However, it is also committed to the belief that all students must be *prepared* to do mathematics—preparation that entails hard work, discipline, commitment, and sacrifice. Due to its philosophy and its success, the Valdes Program has earned a place of distinction in the Elizabeth Union High School District's academic community. It is a program to which many of the participants in this study refer.

Analysis of the Data

All respondents were affiliated with the Elizabeth District. Three surveys were administered to each of five groups of respondents: parents, administrators, curriculum leaders, teachers, and students. Most statements are referenced across group delineations. However, some items relate to only a particular group or combination of groups.

All Agree/Disagree survey items were cast as positive statements and aligned with a descending scale ranging from strongly agree (5) to strongly disagree (1). Respondents were instructed to circle only one choice on the survey, the results were entered into a computer by hand, and tabulated using commercial software.

When the study examines the level of agreement among groups of the PACTS alliance, discussion will focus only on positive (agree and strongly agree) responses. All responses are represented in terms of a percentage of all respondents. In some cases, the results being discussed are represented graphically. Results are reviewed in the following order:

1. An assessment of changes made to district's mathematics curriculum in response to 1985 *California State Mathematics Framework*.

2. The results of the educator survey as they relate to items gleaned from the 1985 *Framework*.

3. The results of the student survey: comparing the responses of those students in classes in existence before the 1985 *Framework* to responses of those students in classes created after the 1985 *Framework*.

4. The results of the parent survey.

5. The results of all survey as they relate to the PACTS alliance.

Interwoven throughout discussions of survey results are respondents' comments, questions, and suggestions on the various issues.

The Framework of Change

The Curriculum

The concept of change was not new to the Elizabeth Union High School District. As it was for the nation as a whole, in the Elizabeth Union High School District the 1980s could be referred to as the decade of change. During 1980-81 school year, the three largest student population in term of ethnicity in the district were White (42.7%), Hispanic (31.7%), and Asian/Pacific Islander (12.9%). Asian and Pacific Islander were, at the time, grouped in district reports. By the end of the decade, the similar figures were: Hispanic (35.2%), Asian/Pacific Islander (34.7%), and White (21.6%). The order of the three largest student groups had changed.

Along with the change in its student population, came all the concerns which confront a district which must serve a diverse student population. The effort to modify its curriculum to meet the needs of this diverse population has been ongoing in the district over the past decade.

In 1987, in response to the *California State Mathematics Framework*, Math A and Math B courses were given "pilot status" by the Instructional Policy Committee in the Elizabeth Union High School District to replace Introduction to Algebra (SAC Interview, 1994). Since then, this experimental curriculum has become infused in the mathematics curriculum at each of the school sites in the district. Of the 602 mathematics courses during the 1993-94 school year, only 13 (2.2%) were Introduction to Algebra. However, the growth of Math A to prominence in the district was not without opposition. Many teachers in the district could not see the wisdom of replacing a single algebra preparatory course with two experimental courses which had no prerequisites skills or entry requirements, little apparent structure, and were too cumbersome to manage or to offer during the summer; hence, difficult to make up if failed. That notwithstanding, the mathematics curriculum in the Elizabeth Union High School District did change. However, the change to the mathematics programs in the district was not uniform, consistent, or across the board.

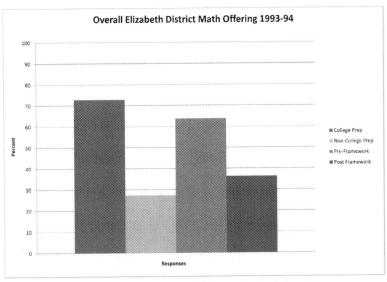

Figure 2 Overall Elizabeth Union High School District Math Course Offerings 1993-94.

Overall District Offerings Of the 602 mathematics courses offered in the Elizabeth Union High School District during the 1993-94 school year, 72.8% (438) are college preparatory classes, and 27.2% (164) are not. Of the 602 courses offered in the district, 63.8% (384) were offered in the district prior to the 1985 *Framework* (pre-*Framework,* and 36.2% (218) are new (post-*Framework*) (see Figure 2).

Type Of the 438 college preparatory courses offered in the district during the 1993-1994 school year, 343 (78.3%) were offered in the district prior to the 1985 *California State Mathematics Framework* (pre-*Framework*), and only 95 (21.7%) are new (post-*Framework*). Of the 164 non-college preparatory courses, 41 (25%) remained that were offered in the district prior to the *Framework,* and 123 (75%) are new or have been introduced to the district in response to, or because of, the *State Framework* (see Figure 3).

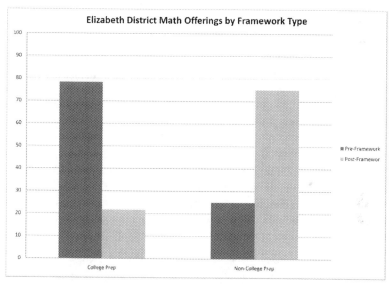

Figure 3 **Elizabeth Union High School District Math Course Offering by FRAMEWORK TYPE.**

Textbooks and Materials Finally, from site to site and even within a particular site, the textbooks and materials used in the district mathematics courses vary; but, nowhere is the variance more evident than in the new, non-college preparatory, post-*Framework* curriculum. Of the 103 sections of Math A offered in the district, four different textbooks or combination of textbooks and district-made materials are used. Of the twenty sections of Math B, again four different textbooks or combination of textbooks and district-made materials are used. In many cases, the textbooks used in Math B is the same as the one used in Math A, or the course it was to replace: Introduction to Algebra. The non-college preparatory courses recommended by the *Framework* are offered throughout the Elizabeth Union High School District without clear guidelines or structure.

On the other hand, in the new college preparatory courses introduced to the district's mathematics curriculum, textbooks and course materials are consistent from site to site. In the only two instances where the materials vary, it is to accommodate computer assisted learning. Although a number of college preparatory classes infused some of the pedagogy advocated by the *Framework*—cooperative learning, manipulatives, and increased use of calculators—it is apparent that the greatest impact of the changes to the mathematics curriculum in the Elizabeth Union High School District is experienced by those students in the non-college preparatory, post-*Framework* classes.

Educators' Perspective

Administrators, Curriculum Leaders, Teachers.

To measure the perceived impact of the *Framework* on the Elizabeth Union High School District's mathematics curriculum by its staff, nine statements were taken ***directly*** from the *Framework* and placed on the educators' survey. Of the nine items, seven related to specific school or district concerns. Those seven items were not placed on parent or student surveys. In addition to two background items, the results of those seven items are discussed in the following paragraphs.

The response rates among the Elizabeth District's policymakers were quite high. Eighty percent (80%) of the administrators, 86% of the curriculum leaders, and 73% of the teachers responded to the educators' survey and the percentages of responses from each of the ten school sites were balanced.

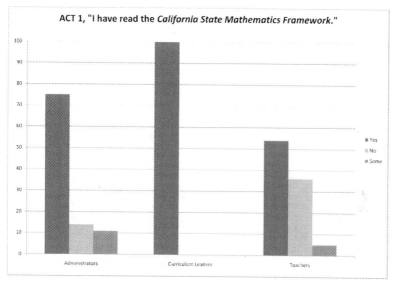

Figure 4 ACT 1, "I have read the *California State Mathematics Framework*."

Seventy-five percent (75%) of the administrators who respond to the survey indicated that they have read the *California Mathematics Framework*, 14% have not, and 11% indicate that they have read some of the *Framework*. All (100%) of the curriculum leaders indicate that they have read the *Framework*. Of the teachers who respond, 54% indicate that they have read the *Framework*, 36% have not, and 5% indicate that they have read some of it (see Figure 4). The researcher should note here that even though the survey did not list "some" as a response option, many respondents felt compelled to write it in.

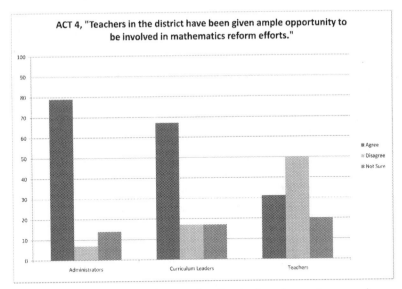

Figure 5 ACT 4, "Teachers in the district have been given ample opportunity to be involved in mathematics reform efforts."

The *Framework* called on mathematics teachers throughout the state to participate in the change process. Teachers were encouraged to create projects, design units, attend workshops, conduct in-services, and participate in professional development activities. Seventy-nine percent (79%) of all administrators in the Elizabeth Union High School District think teachers have been given ample opportunity to be involved in mathematics reform efforts, 67% of the curriculum leaders think so, and, 31% of the mathematics teachers concur (see Figure 5). Some teachers acknowledged that opportunities for school staff to get together have been made available, but expressed concern as to how the time was allocated. One teacher states, "Almost all our in-service time is taken up by special school planned in-services or other special needs—very little time for math(ematics)." Another teacher adds:

> I see the main problem as the district and administration have come up with an idea and instead of testing it or even asking teachers, they

are forcing their ideas of reform on the students and teachers. I feel as a teacher totally powerless and forced to teach what I do not believe in. Convince me first and train me or I cannot help the students. I have been neither convinced nor trained for next years [*sic*] changes (I have gone to Equity 2000 training, but it was a waste of time).

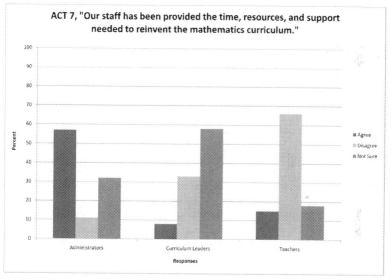

Figure 6 ACT 7, "Our staff has been provided the time, resources, and support needed to reinvent the mathematics curriculum."

To accomplish "genuine change in schools," the *Framework* acknowledges that "time, resources, and problem solving will be needed to reinvent the curriculum and thereby serve all students well." When asked whether staff members in the district have been provided the time, resource and support needed to bring about effective change in the district, the educators of the district are divided. More teachers disagree (67%) that they have been provided the time necessary to "reinvent the mathematics curriculum" than administrators who agree (57%); an approximate equal number (58%) of curriculum leaders are not sure (see Figure 6). One administrator writes, "I have a problem with the word 'reinvent.' I don't see this process as reinventing, but I do feel the teachers have had enough time to make necessary changes."

When asked about the changes that have been made in the district's mathematics curriculum, administrators, curriculum leaders, and teachers express very different views. One of the goals of mathematics reform in the nation, and certainly in the state, was to make mathematics accessible to all students; to increase each student's "mathematical power." The *Framework* stated that many of its recommendations "are motivated by concern for equity—giving every student in California fair access to mathematics education." State guidelines explaining the link between the new Math A course and Algebra I stressed that a major goal of the Math A course was to get students to like mathematics and to see themselves succeeding at it. After their Math A experience, students "would come away with a new appreciation for mathematics" and become *mathematically powerful* students able "to merge with the college preparatory mathematics sequence." The ultimate goal was to increase the number of "underrepresented minority students" in college preparatory classes.

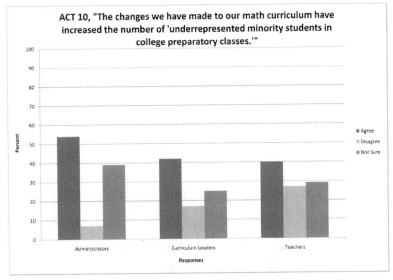

Figure 7 ACT 10, "The changes we have made to our math curriculum have increased the number of of 'underrepresented minority students in the college preparatory classes.'"

Of the educators who responded, 54% of the administrators think that the changes made to the mathematics curriculum has increased the number of "underrepresented minority students" in the college preparatory classes, however, only 42% of the curriculum leaders think so, and still less, 40%, of the teachers agreed (see Figure 7). Because some schools in the district had simply eliminated all remedial mathematics classes and placed all their incoming freshmen in beginning algebra (a directive the district later mandated for all schools during the 1994-95 school year), some teachers questioned any attempt to quantify an increase in the number of minority students in these classes. As one teacher comments:

> The elimination of most Math I/Mastery (*remedial*) mathematics classes and the forced concept of putting 100% of all incoming 9th grade students in Algebra IA classes, ignoring ability levels, lack of prior student preparation in many cases, lack of coordination with feeder schools, and ignoring feeder school recommendations and testing results for individual students, is an ill-conceived and poorly planned policy. Students should be encouraged to go as far as possible, as quickly as possible, but "force" doesn't often accomplish a lot. I don't think failing Alg(ebra) IA is better than getting an A or B is a lower level class and improving self-esteem, as one board member claimed.

Another teacher states, "What is a statistic if kids don't comprehend?" One curriculum leader thought it unreasonable at this time to even pose the question. This curriculum leader writes, "unfair question since we continually have more and more underrepresented minorities."

Even though many educators were not able (or willing) to make any quantitative assessment on the number of minority students in the college preparatory classes, the research delves further to see if educators were able (or willing) to make a qualitative evaluation of the nature of the work these students were doing in their current mathematics classes.

The *Framework* points out that to achieve the goal of an increasing number of minority students in college preparatory classes, courses have to be developed in which assignments are demanding, engaging, and accessible to a wider variety of students. The *Framework* goes on to state that in new programs called for "students will be asked to do more work and take on the responsibility for organizing and revising their work outside of class." Students will need to develop "a mathematical work ethic that requires self-discipline and effort to meet a high-quality standard" (p. 13).

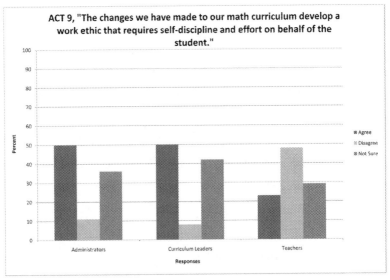

Figure 8 ACT 9, "The changes we have made to our math curriculum develop a work ethic that requires self-discipline and effort on behalf of the student."

When asked whether the changes made to their mathematics curriculum helped to develop a work ethic that required self-discipline and effort on behalf of the students, fifty percent (50%) of administrators and one-half (50%) of the curriculum leaders thought the changes had; however, only 23% of the teachers thought so (see Figure 8). One teacher comments:

I feel too little emphasis is being placed upon the student in all this mathematics reform. In fact, changes seem to be moving the student away from being rigorous and responsible about learning mathematics. Other countries do quite well in traditional settings—they just expect more from students.

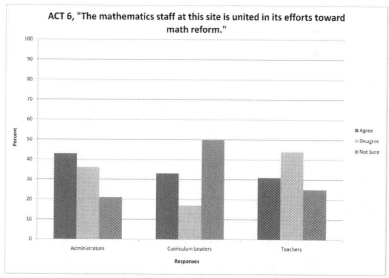

Figure 9 ACT 6, "The mathematics staff at this site is united in its efforts toward math reform."

One administrator warns, "We need to ensure that mathematics reform will prepare students for college. The mathematics reform needs to include programs that will cause students to spend more time studying."

The effect of recent changes to the mathematics curriculum is perhaps the one issue that has caused the greatest amount of dissension among mathematics staff members in the Elizabeth District in recent years. When asked about staff unity at their site, the positive response rate from each group of educators is less than 50%. Forty-three percent (43%) of the site administrators think that their staff is united in its efforts toward mathematics reform;

33% of the curriculum leaders think so; and, 31% of the teachers (see Figure 9). Many teachers view the changes to the district's mathematics curriculum as unnecessary and are resistant to change. As one teacher notes:

> Questions on this survey were done with the whole school in mind. Approximately 1/2 of the [*site*] staff has made a real genuine effort to reform and change mathematics education, while the other has resisted any efforts to do so.

Here, an administrator expresses another view:

> Like always, the begining [*sic*] of a change is a very difficult task. We are just coming to grips with the fact that we are going to change our presentation of mathematics to our students. As the staff excepts [*sic*] this change, it will begin to flourish. Top down directives do not work. The staff must buy into the change. They must also see the need for the change.

The *Framework* acknowledges that support for change on everyone's part is necessary before "positive change can take root." However, many teachers in the district express frustration regarding how little input they think they have in decision-making processes in regard to mathematics reform. Many teachers do see the mathematics reform effort as "top-down" policy about which they have little say. One teacher writes:

> I feel that any and all changes in the mathematics curriculum are basically dictated to the schools from the District Office. The schools, mathematics departments, and individual teachers have little if any say, in what we are doing. Math reform must come from the teachers. They must "own" it or it will not work.

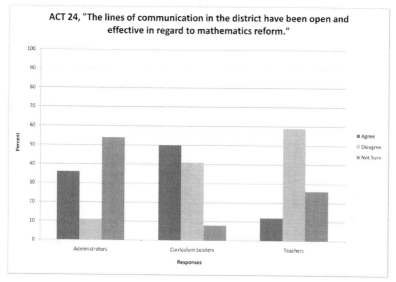

Figure 10 ACT 24, "**The lines of communication in the district have been open and effective in regard to mathematics reform.**"

Only twelve percent (12%) of the teachers who responded to the survey think the lines of communication in the district are open and effective in regard to the mathematics reform movement, 36% of the administrators and 50% of the curriculum leaders think so (see Figure 10). While poor communication is cited by many as one of the leading causes of ineffective mathematics reform in the district, one administrator had this to say:

> Sometimes your choices weren't adequate for me. The best to #20 would have something to do with instructional format. The reason for the lack of reform has less to do with communication, opportunity, and time than it does with tradition & the overwhelming inertia of the system.

This leads to the next topic of investigation.

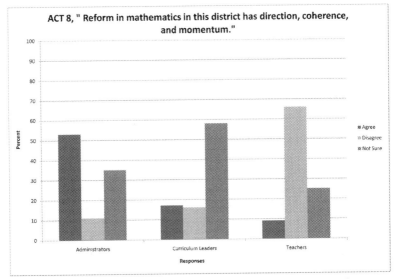

Figure 11 ACT 8, "Reform in mathematics education in this district has direction, coherence, and momentum."

The 1992 *California State Mathematics Framework* heralded "the momentum toward reform" signaled by national, state, and local initiatives. It pointed out that the use of computers and calculators is common; and that innovations in student assessment such as increased use of open-ended questions and portfolios are finding their way into classrooms. Indeed, the new *Framework* proclaimed, "reform in mathematics education has direction, coherence, and momentum" (p. 2). This statement was posed to the educators in the Elizabeth Union High School District to get their "district perspective."

Indeed, 54% of the administrators who respond think that the reform movement in the district has direction, coherence, and momentum. However, only 18% of the curriculum leaders, and a mere 9% of the teachers share this view (see Figure 11). One teacher writes:

> The lack of leadership on the district level as well as the school is very evident: the spending of money (and grants) and the lack of coordination of feeder schools. [*This site*] is consider [*sic*] old fashion (look

at the scores in Math). I thought a building started with a good foundation and not the second or third story. The new mathematics should have been in place at the lower level long before. Some middle schools have done nothing or very little to insure wanted success at the high school level.

Another teacher points out, "Each Elizabeth Union High School District school is an entity unto itself when it comes to mathematics reform—there is virtually no district cohesiveness." An administrator states:

> The major push that is occuring [*sic*] now in the District should have started years ago. No one wanted to make a decision and enforce it. Math A was a perfect example—it was handled very poorly. Also, if you want people to change, you need to convince them it is needed and then train them. We have been too slow on this.

This chart, more than any other, shows the schizophrenic nature of change among the policymakers who must orchestrate it in this district, or any other, for that matter: ***Administrators with one perspective, teachers with another, and curriculum leaders, acting as liaisons between these two agents, stuck and "not sure" in the middle.***

The Students' Perspective

Curriculum changes, of course, do not take place in a vacuum. Each change of class, textbook, course, or methodology of instruction made in response to the 1985 *Framework* impacted students in a very real and personal way. The discussion now focuses on the students' perspectives of the changes made to the Elizabeth Union High School District mathematics curriculum in recent years.

Ten classes at each of ten high schools in the Elizabeth Union High School District were given student surveys. Whenever possible, classes were selected on the bases of being college preparatory or not, a pre-*Framework* class or not, and whether they were representative of a particular level of the mathematics class offered in the district or not. An attempt was made at each school site to survey a mathematics class of each level. Because the researcher relied solely upon the teachers to volunteer their class to be a part of the study, in a few instances (usually when tests or other activities were scheduled), permission was not granted. Therefore, not all class levels at each school site were surveyed.

Of the 100 classes in the Elizabeth Union High School District surveyed, 56 (56%) of them were college preparatory (cp) classes and 44 (44%) were not (ncp). Two thousand, one hundred, sixty-four (2164) students were in these classes: 1314 (61%) were college preparatory students and 850 (39%) were not. Finally, of the 100 classes surveyed, 49 (49%) were taught in the district prior to the 1985 *Framework* and 51 (51%) were introduced to the district's mathematics curriculum as a result of, or in response to, guidelines put forth in the *Framework*. As noted before, the researcher will refer to mathematics classes in the district before the 1985 *Framework* as pre-*Framework classes* and classes introduced to the district's mathematics curriculum after the 1985 *Framework* as post-*Framework* classes. Overall, a district-wide balance in the number, type [cp, ncp, pre-*Framework,* post-*Framework*], and ability level of the classes surveyed was achieved.

The following results of the student surveys compare the responses of all students, to those pre-*Framework* students, and to those of post-*Framework* students. The researcher recognizes that these three groups are inherently different and are made up of students of varied mathematics backgrounds, skills, and abilities; some may say "different kids." However, one of the objectives of this study was to explore those differences to determine whether the "inherent" differences translate into vastly different experiences, perspectives, or inequities on the part of Elizabeth Union High School District students.

Student-School Relations The first question relates specifically to each student: Whether or not they liked mathematics. Forty-eight percent (48%) of all the students surveyed say that they liked mathematics. This figure rises to 55% when asked of students in classes taught in the district prior to the 1985 *Framework*, but drops to 40% when asked of students in classes created after the *Framework* (see Figure 12).

In a recent study conducted by another researcher in the district, it was reported that a student's attitude about mathematics did not change significantly over the course of the year (Lorenzen, 1992). So, if a student entered a course in the fall with a negative attitude toward mathematics, his or her attitude did not improve with the new curriculum and teaching practices advocated by the *California State Framework*. The use of manipulatives, cooperative learning, calculators and the diverse subject matter of the new curriculum made no difference in student attitude (Lorenzen, 1992). This research was conducted in the spring; therefore, the attitude reported here by the students is either one they had coming into the course the previous fall, or one they had developed over the course of the year. At any rate, classes formed based on guidelines espoused by the *State Framework*—despite their intent—do not increase students' appreciation for mathematics.

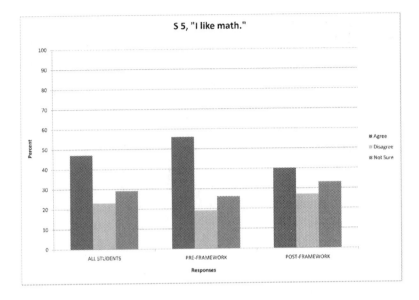

Figure 12 S 5, "I like math

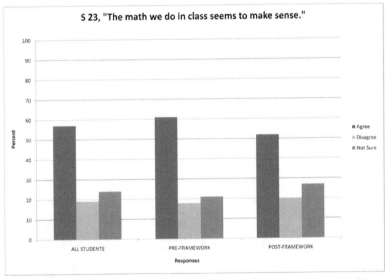

Figure 13 S 23, "The math we do in class seems to make sense."

A major aspect of the new curriculum advocated by the 1985 *Framework* is that it should be divided into large chunks called *units.* At the core of each unit there would exist strands or unifying ideas which take weeks to develop. Mathematics would be given the breadth and depth it needed to relate to the student's real-life experiences. Mathematics would have contextual meaning; it would make sense. Fifty-seven percent (57%) of the students surveyed think that the mathematics they do in class makes sense. Again, that figure does not improve in post-*Framework* classes. In those classes, 52% of the students think the mathematics they do makes sense, as opposed to 61% in the pre-*Framework* classes (see Figure 13). Of course, in light of responses to student question 5 (S, 5), this may seem reasonable. On the one hand, one can argue that because these students do not like mathematics—and are less prepared to do mathematics—they would naturally find it more difficult to understand what is done in class. There is little wonder, then, that what is done in class does not make sense. As one college prep student points out, "I am not doing well in Calculus because I don't do my homework, so the mathematics doesn't make sense. When I do my work, then I understand." On the other hand, one might conclude that the curriculum is at fault for not getting students to see the need to do mathematics. As a student in a non-college preparatory class states, "The packets which we are currently using not only confuse me but have no meaning on anything in my personal life. There are no examples and some of the problems are downright childish."

The Parents' Perspective

The study now introduces the parents to the analysis before going on to examine topics as they relate to parent-school and parent-student relations in the Elizabeth District.

Parent surveys were mailed to 500 parents of Elizabeth Union High School District students. Stamped, self-addressed, envelopes were provided by the researcher for the return of the survey. The mailing list of parents was generated from student rosters of the classes that had already been surveyed; that is, these were parents of students who also participated in the study. This was done so that *questions* cross-referenced on the parent and on the student surveys would have cross-referenced *respondents* as well. Seventy-seven (77) out of 500 (15%) of the parent surveys were returned. Although this number is small, each school site and class level was represented. The following analyses of the first two survey questions offer possible rationales for the low parent survey return rate.

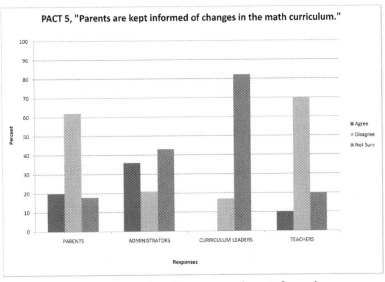

Figure 14 PACT 5, "Parents are kept informed of changes in the math curriculum."

Parent-School Relations Schlechty in *Schools for the 21st Century*, (1990) notes, "Sometimes all they (parents and community leaders) want is some attention and acknowledgement that they too are important and deserving to be taken into account" (p. 95). As we see in Figure 14, a majority of the parents in the Elizabeth Union High School District who responded to the survey do not feel that they have been "taken into account." In fact, there is general agreement among all respondents that parents are not keep informed of what is happening in the schools concerning mathematics curriculum reform. Only thirty-six (36%) of the administrators think parents are kept informed, while 10% of the teachers think so, and *no* curriculum leader thinks so—though 82% are not sure. Only 20% of the parent respondents think they are kept informed of mathematics changes compared to 62% who feel they are not (see Figure 14). It is understandable, then, that parents did not overwhelmingly respond to what they perceived as district request for input on curriculum matters about which they have long felt slighted or uninformed. One parent states, "I've never been informed about mathematics reform before." Another adds, "Better information on this subject given [*sic*] to parents. Most parents are in the dark because of a lack of communication—and information!"

Schlechty (1990) also notes that "parents who are satisfied with their own child's progress in school seldom concern themselves with data that other children are not doing well" (p. 94). One Elizabeth Union High School District parent supports this view when she notes, "I am content with my son's mathematics education, so I have not become involved with pursuing how the overall mathematics is run."

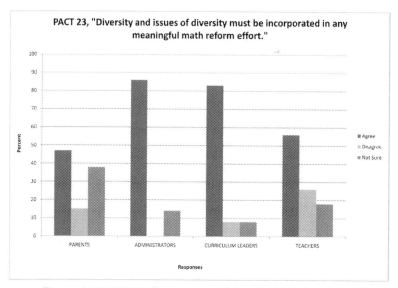

Figure 15 PACT 23, "Diversity and issues of diversity must be incorporated in any meaningful math reform effort."

The results illustrated in Figure 15 explore another aspect of parent-school relations. Only 47% of the parents think that issues of diversity must be included in any meaningful mathematics reform effort. One parent comments, "Diversity of what? Math concepts remain universally the same." And another parent adds, "Math needs to be taught."

Educators viewed the statement in broader terms. Eighty-six percent (86%) of the administrators and 83% of the curriculum leaders think that issues of diversity must be incorporated in the mathematics reform efforts. One administrator notes, "Hispanics and African-American students are not [*sic*] being included." Although, only 56% of the teachers agree, one teacher notes:

> Sp(ecial) Ed(ucation) Math is continuously and consistently left out of any reform movement. Special Ed(ucation) should have many resources and manipulatives available to them than currently is. The Dep(ar)t(ment) doesn't even have textbooks let alone anything else. They are seldom asked for input from the reg(ular) Math Dep(ar)t(ment) even though a good number of our students are mainstreamed.

Indeed, the issue of diversity is as broad for some as it is narrow for others—it is diverse. Yet, it is perhaps best articulated by this student who writes, "I think if there were diverse ethnicity in my Calculus class, I would feel like I belong there. Sometimes I feel out of place and I am afraid to ask a question."

Parent-Student Relations.

> I think most of the reform efforts will have a "watering down" effect on the curriculum. Students need to apply themselves. More and more needs to be done through parent and home. Teachers cannot be all (i.e. substitute parents) and teach the curric(ulum) besides.
>
> --Elizabeth District Teacher

Effective schools involve parents in their children's learning and their school life. Adults need to talk to children about school, and stress the importance of school by providing a supportive learning environment in the home ("The national," 1991). According to teachers in a Child Trends survey, parent involvement is the most important factor in children's learning (Jacobs, 1994). The following questions were designed to examine how parents and students in the Elizabeth Union High School District perceive their parent-student relations. The researcher recognized the sensitive nature of this topic and did not seek to delve into deep personal and psychological issues. The goal was merely to shed some light, however superficially, on an aspect of education reform many view as critical in any serious effort to improve American schools. As one student puts it, "I think better education starts with the family environment. Support from the people at your home is vital to your self-esteem and wanting to learn."

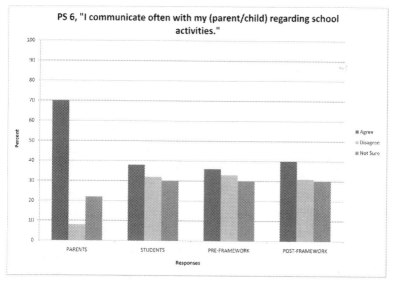

Figure 16 PS 6, "I communicate often with my (parent/child) regarding school activities."

The study of parent-student relations in the Elizabeth District begins with a somewhat paradoxical result. When asked whether they communicate often with their child/parent regarding school activities, 70% of the parents indicate that they communicate often with their child, whereas only 38% of the students indicate they communicate often with their parent (see Figure 16). The student responses were consistent whether they were in a pre-*Framework* or post-*Framework*. The researcher will not attempt to make more of this than there is given that the parent-student responses are not paired one to one. However, one explanation could be that the respondents, because of generational differences, may have very different ideas as to what constitutes "communication." And two, for many students it may not be "cool" to say that you communicate with your parents—even if you do. Perhaps this is an area for further research.

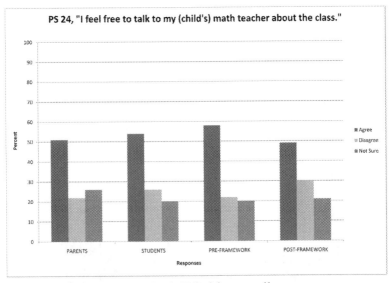

Figure 17 PS 24, "I feel free to talk to my
(child's) math teacher about the class."

An examination of the reported level of communication between the parent and teacher is consistent with the reported level between the student and teacher. Fifty-one percent (51%) of the parent respondents indicate that they feel free to talk to their child's mathematics teacher about the class. However, one parent remarks, "But he never returned my calls." Fifty-four percent (54%) of the student respondents indicate that they feel free to talk to their mathematics teacher about the class. The student responses to this question increase to 58% in classes created prior to the *Framework*, whereas it decreases to 49% in those classes created after the *Framework* (see Figure 17). A student writes:

> What is taught in mathematics classes does not need to be changed, but some of the teachers do. We need teacher who understand and who are ok [*sic*] asking questions. Some past teachers discourage students asking questions by the way they act.

The dynamics of student-teacher relations is one of the leading, and most examined, factors which contribute to student achievement. Educational research has also demonstrated the importance of parental involvement, but most contacts of parents with schools have been superficial (Henderson, 1987; Peterson, 1989).

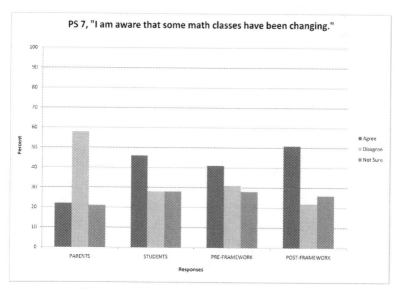

Figure 18 PS 7, "I am aware that some math classes have been changing."

The results of our next question are consistent with previous findings. Only 22% of the parent respondents report that they were aware that some mathematics classes in the district have been changing. This is consistent with the earlier result that only 20% of parents report that school personnel keep them informed of changes in the mathematics curriculum (see Figure 18). One parent comments, "Most answers are not based on knowledge I have regarding this, but opinions. I am totally unaware of any reform efforts being made." The level of awareness of class changes by students overall is understandably higher than that of their parents; yet, only 46% of the students indicate that they are aware that mathematics classes have been changing. As one would expect, the level of awareness is somewhat higher in the post-*Framework* classes than it is in the pre-*Framework* classes: 51% compared to 41%. The comments from students on this issue represented many points of views; from students who like their classes to those who hate them; from those who are aware of changes in the curriculum to those who are not. One confused young man perhaps speaks for many when he writes:

> What would you reform mathematics into? Math just needs to be explained better in unique ways. Unless I do not see what you see. From my point of view I don't know what I should be seeing. But I guess that's me.

As documented earlier, more students in the college preparatory classes are unaware of changes in the mathematics curriculum than students in non-college preparatory classes. Most college preparatory classes in the district have been largely unaffected by current reform efforts (see Figure 3). On many campuses this has lead to dual mathematics curricula: one curriculum that has undergone major change in recent years, and another that has remained largely unchanged.

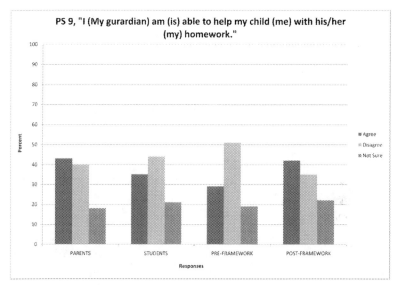

Figure 19 PS 9, "I (My guardian) am (is) able to help
my child (me) with his/her (my) homework."

Parents depend on the schools to educate their children. Parents, the child's first and lifelong teachers, find it increasingly difficult to assist them, especially in mathematics, as they progress in their education. Only 43% of the parent respondents indicate that they are able to assist their child with their mathematics homework; an approximate equal number (40%) indicate that they cannot. The student responses to this question support this finding. Overall 35% of the students indicate that their guardians are able to assist them with their homework, whereas 44% said that they cannot help. The figures are significantly different in pre- and post-*Framework* classes. In the pre-*Framework* classes, 29% of the students report that their parents can help, whereas 51% say that their parents cannot help. In post-*Framework* classes the figures are 42% and 35% respectively (see Figure 19). One student writes, "I can never get help at home in mathematics because my mom does not know how to do mathematics. I don't seem to get it the way my teacher explains it especially when she doesn't help me." Frustrated parents offer a number of solutions to this problem. One parent comments, "I think you should require more tutoring." Another adds:

> I feel the schools should offer more summer classes for mathematics to not only the one's [*sic*] who need it but also to those who seek to enhance their mathematics education. I feel that summer school is a great time for a student to focus on one subject and learn more without worrying about his/her other classes.

The study now addresses a rather sensitive but important aspect of parent-student relations: the need for safe supporting learning environment. With no intentions of being invasive, the survey asks both parents and students whether a safe, quiet study environment exists. Across the board, the responses are affirmative. Seventy-nine percent (79%) of the parents indicate that their child has a safe, quiet place to study. The student respondents affirm this result. Overall, 64% of the students indicate that they have a safe learning environment. This figure is not significantly different for pre-and post-*Framework* classes: 65% and 62% respectively (see Figure 20). Although there is a 15% difference between the responses of the parents and the responses of the students, the researcher acknowledges that there was some confusion on the part of students as to how to interpret this question. Some students were not sure whether the question referred to the home or school environment, and the researcher did not want to influence their response; so it was left to each respondent to interpret and answer the question in his or her own way. The objective of the statement is served either way; the question remains: Do you have a safe, quiet place to study? And, at any rate, this is one of the strongest areas of agreement among the parents and students across the board.

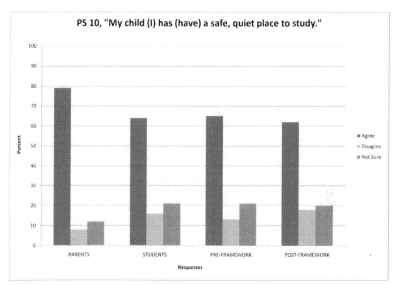

Figure 20 PS 10, "My child (I) has (have) a safe, quiet place to study."

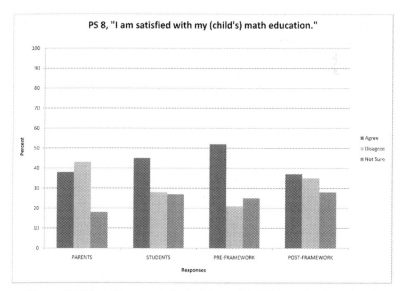

Figure 21 PS 8, "I am satisfied with my (child's) math education."

All parents want the best for their children. The final aspect of parent-student relation that is assessed in this part of the study is the level of satisfaction reported by parents and students in the Elizabeth

Union High School District in regard to their mathematics education experience. Thirty-eight percent (38%) of the parents surveyed express satisfaction with their child's mathematics education. One satisfied parent comments, "My daughter has greatly improved in mathematics over the last 3 years I credit that to the districts and the teachers she has had! I'm pleased." However, a greater number (43%) of the parents surveyed expressed dissatisfaction with their child's mathematics education (see Figure 21). One disgruntled parent railed against the teachers and the system. In part she writes, "I believe the teachers have lost there [*sic*] control of the class and are frustrated because the system doesn't back them up." Another parent comments, "We need to work together for the benefit of all students."

The overall level of satisfaction among students in the district is also below 50%; and the difference in the level of satisfaction between students in the pre-*Framework* classes and the level of those in post-*Framework* classes is also significant: 52% to 37%. Fifteen percent (15%) fewer students in new *Framework* classes are satisfied with their mathematics education than those students in classes taught before the 1985 *Framework*.

PACTS: The Coalition For Change

The study now examines the PACTS relations in the Elizabeth Union High School District. It measures the level of awareness, agreement, and commitment among parents, administrators, curriculum leader, teachers, and students regarding issues that relate to systemic mathematics reforms. It assesses the strength of the alliance and singularity of purpose interwoven between and among these agents of change. In the researcher's view, it is this alliance, or "pact for the benefit of students," that is key to effective and sustainable school reform. It is the "coalition for change."

Because, in this section, the study seeks to examine the level of agreement among the groups of the alliance, the researcher will report, and will discuss, only positive (agree and strongly agree) responses. These responses are represented graphically in terms of a percentage of all respondents. The study will also report and discuss the difference between the responses of pre-*Framework* students and the responses of post-*Framework* students when it is significant. The researcher defines significant as a difference of greater than ten points. The goal here is to address the issue of "inclusion"; to show that because of changes made to the Elizabeth Union High School District mathematics curriculum some students in the district do not feel a part, and are often not a part, of the greater academic community.

Five groups were surveyed: parents, administrators, curriculum leaders, teachers, and students. All group members are affiliated with one of ten high school sites in the Elizabeth Union High School District. Two thousand, three hundred, seventy eight (2,378) respondents participated in the survey; all groups and school sites were well-represented.

Shared Values This examination of the PACTS alliance in the Elizabeth District begins with a discussion of their overall perception of mathematics. There is general agreement among the groups that mathematics is a tough subject which requires organization and discipline to do well. The researcher acknowledges that this question was inspired by a comment made by one of the teachers in the district in response to an introductory letter sent to all teacher respondents. She writes in part:

> I consider mathematics a rigorous, organized, disciplined subject I cannot go along with the reforms that want me to play games with scissors and turn my classroom into a zoo. This violates my philosophy of what mathematics is. Besides, often, the material that is being taught in these styles is often way below the level of what I feel high school should cover.

Based on survey pretest results, the researcher found it necessary to change the word "rigorous" to "tough" so that a greater number of students would have a better understanding of its meaning.

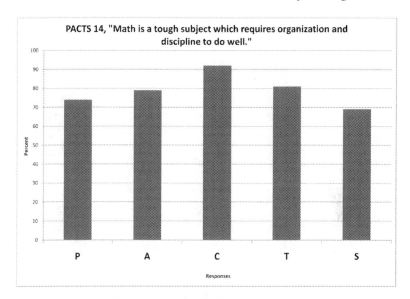

Figure 22 PACTS 14, "Math is a tough subject which requires organization and discipline to do well."

As shown in Figure 22, the overall positive response rate to this
question is high. The positive responses range from a low of 69%
for students to a high of 92% for curriculum leaders. The responses
from students in pre-*Framework* classes differ from that of their
post-*Framework* counterparts by a margin of 13 points; 75% of the
students in pre-*Framework* classes think that mathematics is a tough
subject which requires discipline to do well, compared to 62% of the
students in classes formed after the 1985 *Framework*.

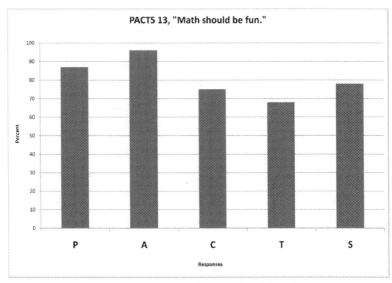

Figure 23 PACTS 13, "Math should be fun."

Although students generally agree that mathematics is "tough," they also want it to be fun. This student expresses the sentiment of many when he writes, "If you change things—make sure the teachers know how to have fun and combine the work and the fun together; believe me, they'll get more kids attention by doing it that way." Here again, there was consensus among the groups regarding this perception of mathematics; 87% of parents, 96% of administrators, 75% of curriculum leaders, and 68% of teachers share the view of 78% of the students (see Figure 23). There is no significant difference in students' opinions based on their class affiliation; all agree that "mathematics should be fun."

On this subject, one parent writes:

> I think teachers need to make mathematics more interesting and relate it to other aspects of life to make mathematics more relevant to the students. The technical instruction is not the only issue—relevance is very important. It is also very important

that the schools monitor the teachers' ability to relate to the class.

Another parent adds:

> Every student is capable of learning mathematics with the proper teaching tools or methods. Teachers must be versatile to the students' needs or level of comprehension, making it interesting and fun to attract the students' attention (every child learns differently).

The researcher notes that the level of agreement reported by the teachers is significantly lower than that of other groups on this issue: 68% of the teachers report that "Math should be fun." Many teachers expressed concern about the danger of correlating "fun" with "learning." S.F. Bourke (1985) reports that "context" is found to be particularly important for the enjoyment of mathematics. He writes, "The more frequent use of small groups of students during lessons and use of teacher worksheets rather than textbooks were associated positively with enjoyment but, at least by implication, negatively with achievement." Teachers recognize that they have a greater responsibility than to just "entertain" students. One teacher writes, "Math should be fun, but not like a game. It should be challenging and its beauty (or wonder) stressed, along with its practical applications."

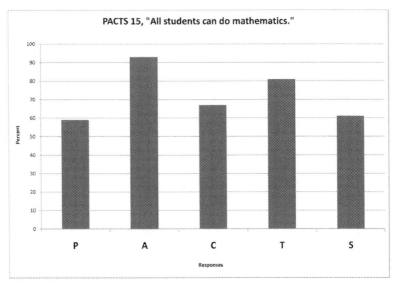

Figure 24 PACTS 15, "All students can do mathematics."

Sense of Purpose Having established that there is general agreement among members of the research group as to their perception of the nature of mathematics, the researcher then explored the questions: "Who can do mathematics?", and "To what end?"

In response to the first of these questions, an overwhelming 93% of the administrators believe that all students can do mathematics, 59% and 61% of the parents and students, respectively, agree (see Figure 24). One administrator writes:

> I believe that we are on the cutting edge of what must be done in the area of mathematics. I become more and more convinced that all students can and will achieve success when and as 'we' truly believe that and teach them accordingly.

As was the case with their perception that "Math should be fun," there is no significant difference between the responses of students in pre-*Framework* and the responses of those in post-*Framework* classes. Teachers and curriculum leaders, too, think that all students can do mathematics; teachers at a positive rate of 81%, curriculum leaders at a positive rate of 67%. The general consensus among all groups is that all students can do mathematics. However, some teachers qualified their responses by stressing that all students can do mathematics—but at different levels and with varying degrees of success.

The first sign of a schism among the alliance for change in the Elizabeth Union High School District surfaces with the next question. It explored whether the mathematics program offered at the various district sites is adequately preparing students for college. Eighty-three percent (83%) of the curriculum leaders in the district thought that it does, but only 42% of the parents agreed. Although 71% of the administrators think favorably of the job schools are doing in this regard, only 54% of the students concur (see Figure 25).

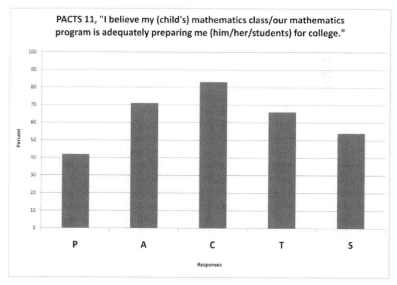

Figure 25 PACTS 11, "I believe my (child's) mathematics class/our mathematics program is adequately preparing me (him/her/students) for college."

The student responses are even more revealing when viewed in the pre-*Framework*/post-*Framework* context: 65% of the students in the pre-*Framework* classes think that their mathematics class is adequately preparing them for college, whereas only 38% of their post-*Framework* peers think so. One exasperated student explains:

> The teachers in the Math B classes have given up on the students. I am going to college. Math B teachers need to encourage the students to learn mathematics. Most Math B students are at the 5th grade level and need to learn NOW not in adult ed(ucation) or later on...

Teachers poll in at a rate of 66% on this issue. One teacher had this to say: "I believe some of the current furvor [*sic*] is purely political and is driven by ethnic changes in the state population. I'm not surprised that the students who aren't pushed toward college don't end up there."

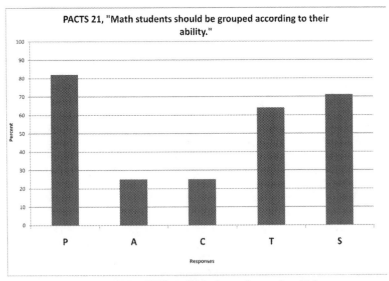

Figure 26 PACTS 21, "Math students should be grouped according to their ability."

The first major "rip" in the fabric of relations among the agents of change in the Elizabeth Union High School District centers around the following issue: What is the best way to deliver mathematics instruction? Eighty-two percent (82%) of the parents and 71% of the students think that mathematics students should be grouped according to their ability and 64% of the teachers in the district support this view (see Figure 26). One parent writes, "I hope you are not changing to classes intermingling all levels of students in class. We just came from that situation in Southern California and it was absolutely frustrating to our son. He was not learning anything." Another parent states, "Math classes should be grouped by ability! Some students hold back others, while some get bored with the slow pace of progress. Both loose [*sic*] interest in mathematics." Administrators and curriculum leaders, however, respond to this question quite differently; in both cases, only 25% of the respondents think that mathematics students should be grouped according to their ability. One administrator hedged and had this to say:

> I believe integrated mathematics with application models are good and that this flavor of change from traditional approaches carries more promise to effectively instruct a diverse group of learning styles. However, I do support retaining a skeleton of the traditional framework and it's [*sic*] sequencing of skills and courses.

As a consequence of the different views about how students should be grouped, there is ambivalence among the respondents as to whether the district's students are placed in the right class. Parents and curriculum leaders are near or at the half-way mark (49% and 50% respectively) on this issue, and administrators are slightly above at 57%. At first glance, teachers appear to be the lone dissenters on this issue—registering 38% level of positive agreement—until one looks more closely at the students' response (see Figure 27).

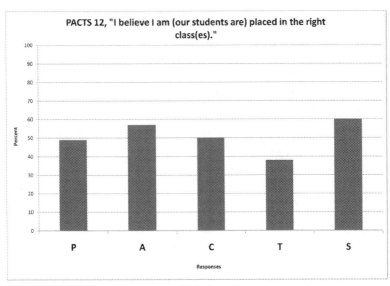

Figure 27 PACTS 12, "I believe I am (our students are) placed in the right mathematics class(es)."

Overall 60% of the students indicate that they believe they are in the right class. However, their level of concern differs significantly when analyzed based on whether they are in a pre-*Framework* or post-*Framework* class. In the classes that were in place prior to the implementation of the 1985 *Framework*, 72% of the students believed they are in the right class; in the classes formed since, or in deference to, the *Framework* only 45% of the students believe they were in the right class—*a 27% difference!* The researcher recognizes that there are cynics who would suggest that this is analogous to an inmate in prison who claims he doesn't belong there—that no one in prison ever believes he or she is in the right place. *But this is not prison.* These are students who simply do not believe they are in a class that is commensurate with their ability, or a class that meets their needs. As one student exclaims, "I am sick of being in the wrong class. I was supposed to be in this class in the 5th grade." On the face of it, many teachers agree.

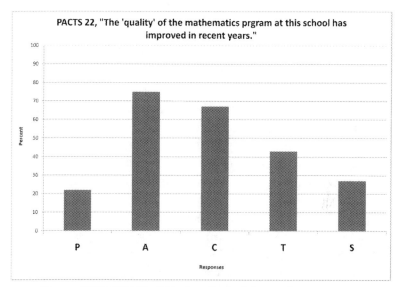

Figure 28 PACTS 22, "The 'quality' of the mathematics program at this school has improved in recent years."

As a consequence of the changes made to the Elizabeth Union High School District's mathematics curriculum, only 43% of the district mathematics teachers think the "quality" of the mathematics program at their school has improved in recent years. The figures for students and parents are even lower: 27% for students, and 22% for parents. Seventy-five (75%) of the administrators and 67% of the curriculum leaders express a different view (see Figure 28). They think their mathematics program has improved. One curriculum leader explains, "Many of these questions can only be adequately answered after a five-year (or more!) timeline has elapsed—any change must show its effects over a long baseline!" However, at least one teacher has reached this conclusion, "I think our Admin(istration) has changed from a working program to a losing program especially for 'low students.' (They) dropped Intro(duction) to Alg(ebra)."

Incorporation of Diversity The 1992 *Framework* echoes the 1985 *Framework* as it reasserts "the goal of mathematical power for all students." The *Framework* goes on to emphatically state that "the recommendations here are motivated by a concern for equity—

giving every student in California fair access to mathematics education." It was this precept which led the researcher to pose the following statement to the participants in the study: "Because the student population in California is changing, we must change the mathematics curriculum." The responses to this statement vary. The responses of 64% of the administrators are positive. The parents and curriculum leaders agree with this statement at response rates of 55% and 53% respectively. Only 41% of the students, and only 27% of the teachers, think that because the student population is changing, change should occur in the mathematics curriculum as well (see Figure 29). Many proponents are quick to point out that the change in the student population in California is not the *only* reason to change the mathematics curriculum; that there are other social and technological reasons as well. As one teacher notes, "We need to bring technology into the mathematics curriculum." But many who opposed questioned whether a changing student population is *any* reason to change the mathematics curriculum. One teacher writes:

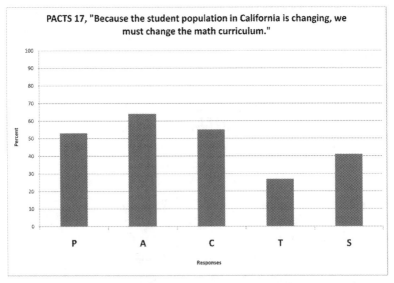

Figure 29 PACTS 17, "Because the student population in California is changing, we must change the math curriculum."

As a black person, I resent the notion that other black people need special accommodation to make it into higher mathematics classes. Personally, I find the mathematics reform movement to be inherently racist. 2 + 2 = 4 whether one is black, white or other. Students should be placed in classes where they can work at an appropriate level and should be required to know something before moving up. Brighter students should not be used to prop up those who don't work as hard. We will teach our brightest that they can get by with little or not work. Ideas like "mathematics reform" explain why so many public school teachers send their children to private schools.

Another teacher concludes, "Change is good. Reason is wrong."

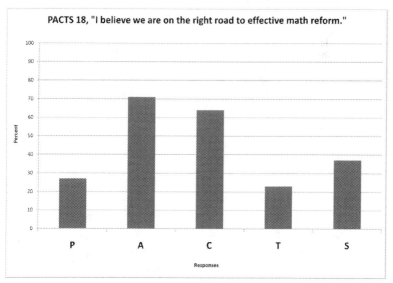

Figure 30 PACTS 18, "I believe we are on the right road to effective math reform."

Shared Vision The agents of change in the Elizabeth Union High School District are torn on the issue as to whether they are "on the right road toward effective mathematics reform." The range of responses on this issue is 48 percentage points (see Figure 30). Seventy-one percent (71%) of the administrators and 64% of the curriculum leaders believe they are "on the right road," compared to 23% of the teachers and 27% of the parents. The students weigh in at 37% on this issue; clearly, the district is divided on this issue. And though there is great dissension in the district about the road to effective mathematics reform, there is general agreement in the district that the path must be found and a road taken.

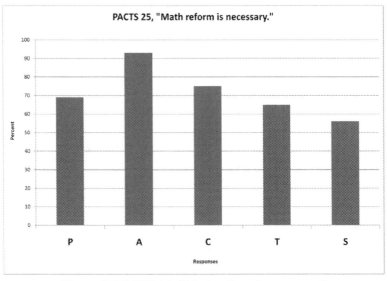

Figure 31 PACTS 25, "Math reform is necessary."

The *California State Mathematics Framework* states, "Math reform is necessary." Generally, the alliance of parents, administrators, curriculum leaders, teachers, and student in the Elizabeth Union High School District agree. Sixty-nine percent (69%) of the parent respondents think "reform of some sort is necessary to advance our students' comprehension of their future." An overwhelming 93% of the administrators think so, and 75% of the curriculum leaders agree. Sixty-five percent (65%) of the teachers indicate that mathematics reform is necessary (see Figure 31). One teacher expounds:

Math reform is necessary. Good teachers are necessary. Creativity and flexibility are necessary. Being able to stop—say, "I've made a mistake" (in pedagogy), regroup, and go on in another direction--is also necessary. But the most important part is parenting. A good parent has made hundreds of thousands of choices in preparing a child for life. Let's allow the parents to bring that expertise into our job as their servants. They want the best for their individual child.

In light of the recent (and prospective) changes in the district, a few teachers expressed a measure of confusion as to how to respond to this statement. Another teacher writes, "Does question 25 mean that the previous reforms need reforming or that the reforms we made were necessary and reform is an ongoing question?" The researcher acknowledges that any response to a statement of this type is suspect in a district undergoing so many changes at the same time: *Framework* reform, Equity 2000, mandated "algebra for all." However, the input from participants on this issue is of interest. Perhaps this is nowhere more evident than in further analysis of the students' results. Although 56% of the students in the district believe that mathematics reform is necessary, the positive response rate (54%) in the classes created in response to (or because of) the *California Mathematics Framework* is nearly as great as the positive response (58%) in classes in existence before the *Framework*. For both groups of students, it seems, math reform is still necessary.

Change: The Means, The Way, The End

This study concludes it analysis of PACTS in the Elizabeth Union High School District with discussions of responses by members of the alliance to three statements specifically designed to measure their perception of the mathematics reform movement along a particular line of reasoning: (a) the means, (b) the way, and (c) the end of change. That is: (a) who or what, in the respondent's view, has the power (*means*) to bring about change; (b) through whom or in what manner (*way*) would it be best to work to bring about change; and (c) what should be the goal or outcome (*end*) of change.

The response choices to each of these three statements are somewhat broad and intentionally reflective. That is, response choice *a* is either *the parent* or reflects a responsibility of a parent; similarly, choice *b* is *the administration* or reflects a responsibility of an administrator; choice *c* is *the curriculum* or reflects an aspect of the curriculum; choice *d* is *the teacher* or reflects a responsibility of a teacher; and choice *e* is *the student* or reflects a responsibility of a student.

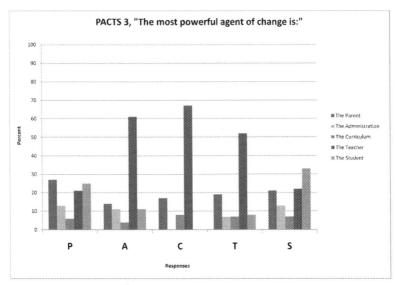

Figure 32 PACTS 3, "The most powerful agent of change is:"

The Means When asked to identify the most powerful agent of change, 61% of the administrators, 67% of the curriculum leaders, and 52% of the teachers choose "the teacher." Parents and students select themselves: 27% of the parents think "the parent" is the most powerful change agent and 33% of the students think "the student" is most powerful. No curriculum leader identifies "the administration" as the most powerful agent of change (see Figure 32). Also of interest here, is how highly the students view themselves—they astutely recognize themselves as "powerful agents of change," and maintain this perspective in the statements which follow.

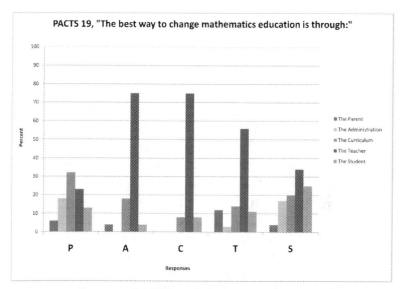

Figure 33 PACTS 19, "The best way to change
mathematics education is through:"

The Way When asked to identify the best way to change mathematics education, again the administrators, curriculum leaders, and teachers chose "the teacher." This time, they are joined by the students. Seventy-five percent (75%) of the administrators and curriculum leaders, 56% of the teachers, and 34% of the students indicate that the best way to change mathematics education is through the teacher (see Figure 33). However, as before, the students recognize themselves as the *next* "best way to change mathematics education." They take personal responsibility for improving their education. The parents think otherwise. Thirty-two percent (32%) of the parents think the best way is through "the curriculum," followed by (23%) who chose "the teacher." Again, as in the PACTS 3 before, "the teacher" is not the overwhelming choice for parents or students as it is for educators. Also of interest, no curriculum leader thinks the best way to change mathematics education was through "the parent"; and no curriculum leader, nor any administrator, thinks that the best way to change mathematics education is through "the administration." "The curriculum," which is currently the engine that drives the *vehicle of change* in the Elizabeth Union High School

District, and the state for that matter, is not thought to be the *best* way to change mathematics education by *any* group of educators.

The End Taken on its own, this question simply seems to indicate that 61% of the administrators, 50% of the curriculum leaders, and 39% of the mathematics teachers believe that students would do better in mathematics if they "saw the need to." However, it was always the intent of the researcher to analyze the response to this question in conjunction with the previous two responses: PACTS 3 and PACTS 19. The phrase "saw the need to" is linked to the curriculum. That is, the phrase "saw the need to" is to suggest that the curriculum makes sense and that it has "contextual meaning" to the student. So, analyzed in light of the result of PACTS 19, the results indicate that educators *do not* believe "the curriculum" currently *is* or *can be* the "best way" to get students "to see the need to" do mathematics. Further, in light of the results of PACTS 20, the results seem to suggest that educators *do* believe it is "the teacher" who must motivate the students and inspire them "to see the need to" do mathematics.

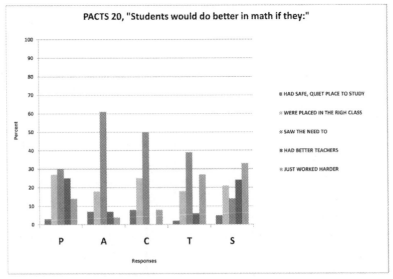

Figure 34 PACTS 20, "Students would do better in math if they:"

Thirty percent (30%) of the parents believe students would do better in mathematics if "they saw the need to." However, an almost equal number of them (27%) also believe that students' performance in mathematics would improve if they were "placed in the right class." Thirty-three percent (33%) of the students believe that they would do better in mathematics if they "just worked harder" (see Figure 34). Again, the researcher thinks it is important to note the students' maturity and sense of responsibility. They perceive of themselves as "masters of their fate" and "powerful agents of change"; perhaps, this is the sort of *empowerment* the *Framework* should seek to nurture. Also of interest, 27% of the teachers think that students would do better in math if they "just worked harder"; conversely, an approximate equal percent of students (24%) think that they would do better in mathematics if they "had better teachers."

Finally, the research suggests that the percentage rate of students who believe that they would do better in mathematics if they were placed in the right class is significantly higher in post-*Framework* classes than it is in pre-*Framework* classes. In the pre-*Framework* class, 17% of the students think they would do better in mathematics if they were in the right class; compared to 27% of the students in the post-*Framework* classes. Again, this seems to indicate that students in post-*Framework* classes do not believe the new curriculum is meeting their needs.

[Before discussing the final question asked of all members of the PACTS alliance, the researcher wishes to acknowledge that many respondents expressed concern with being "forced" to select only one choice from the list: the parent, the administration, the curriculum, the teacher, and the student. In fact, despite instructions to the contrary, a number of respondents circled more than one choice (invalidating their results). They astutely indicated that the most powerful agent of change, and the best way to bring about effective change for the betterment of students in the Elizabeth Union High School District, was through a collaborative effort; that is, PACTS: The Coalition for Change.]

Structural changes, after all, require systems of authority to be altered, systems of reward to be redesigned, and the symbols of power and prestige to be rearranged. Such fundamental changes cannot occur unless those who have control over the resources of the organization (the moral and symbolic resources as well as the financial and physical resources) can be persuaded to use their control in ways to support the change (p. 9).

--Phillip C. Schlechty
Schools for the 21st Century

PACTS: The Coalition For Change The future of the mathematics reform effort in California, and the rest of this nation for that matter, may rest upon the creation of collegial interactions among the various agents of change as has been prescribed above. However, in this district, less than one-third of *any* group of respondents thought that the sense of "community" associated with and, arguably, essential to the success of any collaborative effort has been developed among the members of the PACTS alliance regarding mathematics reform in the district. Only thirty-two percent (32%) of the administrators; and, even lower numbers of parents and students (26% and 25% respectively), think that a sense of community had been developed. Moreover, only 17% of the curriculum leaders and a mere 3% of all teachers express similar beliefs (see Figure 35).

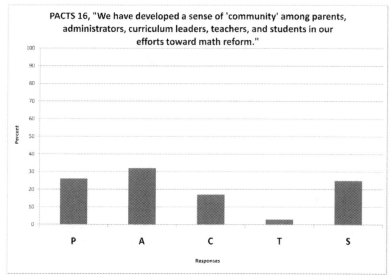

Figure 35 PACTS 16, "We have developed a sense of 'community' among parents, administrators, curriculum leaders, teachers, and students in our efforts toward math reform."

Indeed, this examination of the PACTS alliance in the Elizabeth Union High School District concludes with the sobering acknowledgement of parents, administrators, curriculum leaders, teachers, and students that the "coalition for change" of which we speak, and to which this study has been devoted, like the mythical district itself, ***does not exist!***

Conclusions, Implications, Recommendations

Conclusions

The California State Mathematics Framework has had a profound effect on the mathematics curriculum in the Elizabeth Union High School District. The impact of the changes made by the Elizabeth Union High School District to its mathematics curriculum was felt by its staff, students, and community.

The purpose of this study was to examine the level of agreement among the various agents of change in the Elizabeth Union High School District on issues as they related to the implementation of the *California State Mathematics Framework*. One of its goals was to investigate whether the mathematics curricular changes experienced in the district worked to the betterment of or as a detriment to the students in the district.

The results of the study warrant the following conclusions:

1. Educators in the Elizabeth District have vastly different perspectives on issues that relate directly to the *Framework*. On the one hand, many administrators in the district believed that teachers have been given ample time, resources, and support to revamp the mathematics curriculum; most of the teachers do not; and just as many curriculum leaders are not sure. Although an expressed goal of the new

Framework was to celebrate the "gift of diversity" and to thereby increase the number of minority students in college preparatory classes, most educators in the district cannot say whether this objective has been achieved. Furthermore, in light of other complex curricula changes, many educators doubt that there is a standard by which this objective can be measured. That notwithstanding, most teachers in the district are convinced that the changes that have been made to the mathematics curriculum do not provide students with the work ethic or self-discipline required to do higher mathematics.

2. The overall effect of mathematics reform has been deleterious to the morale, the unity, and the sense of purpose among Elizabeth Union staff. Most survey participants attribute the district's inability to move forward and to effectively change its mathematics curriculum to a lack of direction, poor leadership, and ineffective communication.

3. Over the past decade, the mathematics curriculum in the Elizabeth Union High School district has become splintered and fragmented. In many cases, and at many sites, there exists a dual-curriculum. On the one hand, of the 438 college preparatory mathematics classes in the district, only 21.7% are have been significantly changed, or even affected, by the guidelines put forth by the *Framework*. On the other hand, of the 164 non-college preparatory classes, 75% of them are new to the district—even if some "in name only." Often the same textbooks and materials are used across the new curricula. Not surprisingly, students in these courses report no positive change in their attitude toward mathematics or their understanding of it. Students in the newly formed *Framework* classes are more likely to believe that they are "in the wrong class" as opposed to their

pre-*Framework* counterparts. This perception has led many post-*Framework* students to express great dissatisfaction with their mathematics education; a disposition they share with many Elizabeth District parents.

4. Although most respondents agree that mathematics reform is necessary, there are significant differences in the perspectives of parents, administrators, curriculum leaders, teachers, and students as to the means, the ways, and the ends of change. Whereas educators look to the teachers to effect change, parents and students look to themselves as "the most powerful agent of change." Meanwhile, "the curriculum" continues to be the engine which powers the vehicle of change in the district toward some *ill-defined* goal prescribed by the state.

5. The level of agreement among the members of the PACTS alliance in the Elizabeth Union High School District is greatest on the issues that relate to the "nature of mathematics." Most agree that mathematics is a "tough" subject which requires organization and discipline to do well, and that "it should be fun." However, the level of agreement among the alliance erodes when the focus shifts to other fundamental issues of systemic reform: the delivery of instruction, the lines of communications, or the very basic issue as to whether or not students should be grouped. On the latter of these, the majority of parents, teachers, and students in the district believe that students should be grouped according to their math ability, whereas most administrators and curriculum leaders do not.

Implications

All parents want the best for their children. Along with the dedicated staff members of Elizabeth Union High School District, they work to provide quality education for their children. Many of the problems and challenges faced by the agents of change in the Elizabeth District over the past few years were born out of a sincere effort by district administrators and policymakers to meet, and at times, to unilaterally implement real or perceived state mandates. However, rapidly implemented new structures have led to confusion, ambiguity, conflict, and ultimately to retrenchment (Fullan, 1993). In their haste to embrace mathematics curriculum change, key district policymakers failed to recognize an essential element of educational change. Fullan writes:

> Mandates are important. Policymakers have an obligation to set policies, establish standards, and monitor performance. But to accomplish certain kinds of purposes—in this case, important educational goals—you cannot mandate what matters, because what really matters for complex goals of change are skills, creative thinking and committed action (McLaughlin 1990).

He continues, "Teachers are not technicians"…to prosper "schools must engage state policies (not necessarily implement them literally), if they are to protect themselves from wrongheaded imposition" (p. 129).

You cannot mandate what matters.

Recommendations

As the *Mathematics Framework for California Public Schools* seeks to celebrate "The Gift of Diversity," so must the Elizabeth Union High School District. It must continue to celebrate its rich diversity and tap the human resources which have long contributed to make it the unique district that it is.

Indeed, as stated in the 1992 Framework, "along with the gift of diversity come responsibilities" and "empowering mathematics programs are inclusive." So, too, are *empowering mathematics reform movements*. For years, the parents, administrators, curriculum leaders, and teachers of the Elizabeth Union High School District have worked to provide quality education to its diverse population of students—in and out of the classrooms. Now, as they endure sweeping changes in the district's efforts to embrace math curriculum reforms, there is the overwhelming desire on their part to be included—to know that their views as parents, administrators, mathematics professionals, and students are valued, welcomed, and respected. Only when the district works to make *mathematics reform* "accessible to all," will a sense of equanimity, balance, and direction be restored.

Based on the findings of this study, the following recommendations are made to the policymakers in the Elizabeth Union High School District.

1. Create committees of parents, administrators, curriculum leaders, teachers, and students (PACTS) at each of the ten school sites to review the findings of this study. Coalesce these committees to form a district-wide PACTS to develop and to infuse a sense of "community" and "inclusion" throughout the district—elements essential to effective and sustainable school reform.

2. Reconsider "wrongheaded" impositions by those outside of the district. Instead, work to develop the infrastructure needed throughout the district to meet the needs of its unique and diverse student population.

3. Remember, you cannot mandate what matters. The end of math curriculum reform is not simply to implement real or imagined mandated policies. Refocus mathematics reform policies and efforts to incorporate and to accentuate the "skills, creative

thinking and committed action" of the dedicated parents, administrators, curriculum leaders, and teachers of the Elizabeth Union High School District.

4. **Recognize that *there is simplicity and a beauty to the process, but it is not a simple process.*** *A*dministrators, *c*urriculum leaders and *t*eachers must come and **_act_** together to implement **action plans** which make reform meaningful and real. And, as policymakers, *ACT* as the center of P*ACT*S Coalitions, with the curriculum **_at the core._** After all, the core function of education reform is to better educate our students.

5. Parents and students must be recognized as integral agents in any reform process and not postscripts (ps) in the aforementioned **action plans.** Reform starts with the parents: the child's first teachers who set the tone for the rest of their lives. It ends with the students to whom all the effort and focus must be directed. And, who ultimately, as they recognize, must be motivated and inspired to learn.

In conclusion, until teachers, districts, communities, and administrators, truly learn to work together to make some of these possibilities real for students who represent the diversity of California's multicultural population and, in fact, this nation, another generation of students will be caught up in a new decade of change. Unfortunately, many of them may be caught short.

Indeed, you cannot mandate what matters. What really matters are the **_students_** of the Elizabeth Union High School District, and this nation.

Afterword

This study concludes with the acknowledgment that the PACTS Coalition can be expanded to include other powerful agents of change that have fueled the engines of school reform for decades, and continue to have tremendous impact on students' lives. The composition of these coalitions may vary from district to district, or state to state. However, regardless of their composition, locale, district, or state, these agents of change lay the foundation upon which all schools are built. Their levels of interaction, interplay, and synergistic relationships, as demonstrated here, are ***universal, measurable, and real.*** And each of us, necessarily, plays a role. Education is a community responsibility. Until we accept that, we are just passing the buck (Fortenbaugh, 2010).

- Parents, Policymakers, Politicians
- Administrators, Advocates
- Curriculum Leaders, Community Leaders, Counselors
- Teachers, Trustees
- Students, Superintendents, School Boards

Ultimately, as they are astutely aware, lasting education reform starts with the parents and ends with the students. ***They are the beginning and the end of the PACTS: Coalition for Change, with the curriculum--the education of all students--at its core.***

References

Aratani L. (1994, September 28) Wilson kills class funding; testing hangs in balance: Class funding vetoed; testing uncertain for '95 San Jose Mercury, pp1.

Ball, D.L., & Cohen, D.K. (1990) Policy and practice: An overview Educational Evaluation and Policy Analysis, 12, 233-239.

Berry, B., & Ginsburg, R. (1990) Effective schools, teachers, and principals: Today's evidence, tomorrow's prospects Educational Leadership and Changing Contexts of Families, Communities, and Schools, Eighty-ninth Yearbook of the National Society of Education, Part II Chicago: University of Chicago.

Beyer, L.E. & Apple, M.W., (Eds.) (1988) The curriculum: Problems, politics and possibilities Albany: State University of New York Press.

Bourke, S.F. (1985) The study of classroom contexts and practices Teaching and Teacher Education Australian Council for Educational Research, 1, pp 33-50.

California Board of Education (1985) Mathematics framework for the California public schools, kindergarten through grade twelve Sacrament, CA: California State Department of Education.

California Board of Education (1992) <u>Mathematics framework for the California public schools, kindergarten through grade twelve</u> Sacramento, CA: California State Department of Education.

California Board of Education (1985) <u>Model curriculum standards: Grades nine through twelve</u> Sacramento, CA: California Board of Education.

Cawelti, G. (1993) Conclusion: The search for a system <u>Challenges and Achievements of American Education</u>, 1993 ASCD Yearbook Washington, D.C.: ASCD

Clinton signs into law education reform bill (1994, April) <u>San Jose Mercury</u>, p5E.

Cuban, L. (1993, November 28) Why corporate solutions won't fix school's problems: School, businesses aren't blood relatives <u>The San Jose Mercury</u>, p1C.

Economist (1990, March) <u>Black Americans</u> 314(7644):17-19.

Educational Resources Information Center (1991) <u>Pursuing diversity: Recruiting college minority students</u> (Report NoED 333856) Washington, D.C>: ERIC Clearinghouse on Higher Education(ERIC Document Reproduction NoEDO-HE-90-7)

Elam, S.M. (1990) <u>The 22nd annual Gallup poll of the public's attitudes toward the public schools</u> Phi Delta Kappan, 77(1), 42EJ 413 175.

Elizabeth Union High School District (1993) <u>Academic, personal and social success for all students</u> Northern California District Printing Office.

ERIC Digest (1991) <u>The national education goals: Questions and answers</u> ACCESS ERIC Rockville, MD: Office of Educational Research and Improvement Washington, D.CEDO-AE-91-2.

Executive Office of the President (1990) National Goals of Education Washington, D.CED 319 143.

Fortenburgh, P. (2010, November 7) Clark Kents, not Superman, can save schools <u>The San Jose Mercury</u>, pA14

Fullan, M. (1993) Innovation, reform, and restructuring strategies <u>Challenges and Achievements of American Education</u>, 1993 ASCD Yearbook Washington, D.C.: ASCD.

Geist, P., & Putnam, R. (1994) <u>What about basic skills</u>? <u>Examining learning and change of two teachers</u> Michigan State University Educational Policy and Practice Study.

Grant, S.G., Peterson, P.L., & Shojgreen-Downer, A. (1994) <u>Learning to teach mathematics in context of systemic reform</u> Michigan State University Educational Policy and Practice Study.

Guido, M. (1994, May 16) Chorus fighting new test is louder controversy: Uproar over class echoes through political arena <u>The San Jose Mercury</u>, pp1A.

Henderson, A. (1987) The evidence continue to grow: Parental involvement improves student achievement National Committee for Citizens in Education ED 315 199.

Hodgkinson, H.L. (1983) <u>Guess who's coming to college: Your students in 1990</u> Washington, D.C.: National Institute of Independent Colleges and Universities.

Jacobs, J. (1994, September 15) How to educate your child <u>The San Jose Mercury</u>, pp11B.

Klein, M.F. (ed.)(1991) <u>The politics for curriculum decision-making</u> Albany: State University of New York Press.

Lester, T. (1989) Math A, a brief description California State Department of Education.

Lorenzen, N. (1992) <u>Attitudes toward mathematics of Math A students</u> Unpublished master's thesis, San Jose State University, San Jose, CA.

Mullis, I., Owen, E.H., & Phillips, G.W. (1990) <u>America's challenge: Accelerating academic achievement</u> Princeton, NJ.: Educational Testing Service.

McLaughlin, M. (1990) The rand change agent study revisited <u>Educational Researcher</u>, 19: 11-16.

National Assessment of Educational Progress (1990) The civic report card Princeton, N.J.: Educational Testing Service.

National Commission on Excellence in Education (1983) <u>A Nation at Risk The Imperative for Educational Reform</u> Washington, D.C.: U.S Government Printing Office.

National Council of Teachers of Mathematics (1989) <u>The Curriculum and Evaluation Standards for School Mathematics</u> Reston, Va.: National Council of Teachers of Mathematics.

National Research Council (1989) <u>Everybody Counts: A Report to the Nation on the Future of Mathematics Education</u> Washington, D.C.: National Academy Press.

Oakes, J. (1985)<u>Keeping track: How schools structure Inequality</u> New Haven: Yale University Press.

Oakes, J. (1988) Tracking: can schools take a different route? <u>NEA Today</u>, <u>6</u>, 41-47.

Oakes, J. (1992, May) Can tracking research inform practice? Technical, normative, and political considerations <u>Educational Researcher</u>, 12-21.

Office of Educational Research and Improvement (1991) <u>Pursuing diversity: Recruiting college and minority students</u> (Report NoEDO-HE-90-7) Washington, D.CERIC Clearinghouse on Higher Education(ERIC Document Reproduction Service NoED 333856)

Pajek, E. (1993) Change and continuity in supervision and leadership <u>Challenges and Achievements of American Education</u>(1993)1993 ASCD YearbookWashington, D.C.: ASCD.

Peterson, D. (1989) Parent involvement in the educational process ERIC Clearinghouse on Educational Management ED 312 776.

Schelechty, P. C. (1990) <u>Schools for the twenty-first century: Leadership imperatives for educational reform</u> San Francisco, CA: Jossey-Bass Inc.

Schubert, W.H. (1993) Curriculum reform <u>Challenges and Achievements of American Education</u>(1993)1993 ASCD Yearbook Washington, D.C.: ASCD.

Staff (1984, Fall) Caution! Slippery paths ahead! <u>Mathematics Diagnostic Testing Program</u>, p1.

Subject Area Coordinator (1994) [Elizabeth Union High School District] Unpublished interview.

US Bureau of the Census (1990, September)<u>Money, income, and poverty status in the united states—1989</u> Washington, D.C.: U.S. Government Printing Office.

Bill Collins

"The PACTS Guy!"

Bill Collins is a veteran educator in California public schools. He has taught all levels of mathematics, lead departments, and directed innovative and uniquely successful mathematics programs. Over the course of his career he has been a parent, administrator, curriculum leader, teacher, and student.

He has degrees in mathematics, philosophy, and a Master's Degree in Education. He is a contributing author to one of the leading middle and high school mathematics textbook series in the nation.

He has served as a consultant to the California State Department of Education, wrote for the California Golden State Examinations, and currently serves as an advisor to the City of San Jose's Early Care and Education Commission.

He is the founder and director of The Sisyphus Foundation—a mathematics support organization dedicated to nurturing PACTS Coalitions as they emerge in districts across the nation.

To subscribe to Bill Collins' PACTS newsletter or to order a PACTS review of your program, visit:

www.thesisyphusfoundation.org

Email Bill Collins at: bc@thesisyphusfoundation.org

or

bc@sisyphvs.com

Where "u" can make a difference!

Index

Printed in the United States
by Baker & Taylor Publisher Services